A Spy Called Swallow:
An Enduring Love Story

John Murray

**Foreword, Prologue and Epilogue
by Leeroy and Peter Murray**

First published by W. H. Allen 1978

Published by GB Publishing.org 2017

CBP.

GB Publishing.org

www.gbpublishing.co.uk

To family friend Anita Compton, 'Twinkle', surrogate daughter of 'Pops', who brought great happiness into his life. To the families Murray and Varicopoulous. And a special dedication to our long lost cousin Nicholai who survived being left behind by the Murrays during the late 1930s in Lithuania.

'To the University of Nottingham its Tutors, Staff, and the Students of my year 1972/1973 and those to come.' : John Murray

Acknowledgements

Peter and Leeroy owe much to the support of their wives, Wendy and Michelle. It must be said that Wendy above all supported John and the family for many years. And to the tolerance of their respective children for listening to their life story again and again...and again.

The Murray family's life was perhaps always destined to cross with their now lifelong friend, Margo Picken. It did so in 1963 when Margo met John junior on a student trip to Moscow. She has kept the 'light shining' over the years for the time when Leeroy and Peter would be ready to write about their rich heritage.

Gratitude is expressed to George Boughton and Brenda Marsh for their enthusiasm and encouragement in helping bring this project to fruition.

CONTENTS

1

FOREWORD

Reprinting *A Spy Called Swallow* allowed Leeroy and Peter Murray to complete their father's story about his enduring love for their mother - Nora, the Russian spy. The moment he met Nora, John's life changed irrevocably and dramatically. He may well have had girlfriends before, but up to that point he largely kept to himself, protecting his independent, self-determined lifestyle. As a businessman travelling the Baltic states, his suits, shirts and shoes were usually made-to-measure. He carried gold coins secretly hidden in his belt, readily available and easily exchangeable. He also carried his favourite compact Bayard automatic gun.

John was worldly in his outlook; earned from his rich experiences as a businessman. He went from an employee at a cigarette-making factory in Kovno, Lithuania, to owning his own factory in Riga, Latvia. With his knowledge of languages, he also became a broker for air engine parts, importing them from the UK for clients in Latvia, Norway and Finland. He may even have been involved in arms dealing. His last business address was in Helsinki when World War II broke out.

Whichever country John found himself in, he was easily accepted as part of the expat community, socialising with others at British Embassy events. He also regularly attended the community church services. His was a self-contained understated lifestyle. He operated very much beneath the radar, not one for being showy, or to covet attention. His experiences as a courier from 1939 onwards suited his self-reliance and lone-wolf tendencies. It also drew on his ability to mentally shut-down, ignore everything around him and focus on the task at hand. He was not easily intimidated.

When John met Nora, his independent existence took a very different turn, one that later left his life hanging in the balance. How much he fully understood about Nora's previous life at that time is not known. His uncompromising commitment to her was made when, one evening in November 1941, whilst leaning on the railing of his homeward-bound ship, Temple Arch, docked at Molotovsk Archangel, he watched with incredulity as a lone figure struggled

3

through the blizzard. Against impossible odds, Nora had made it from Moscow to the inhospitable northern ports of Russia simply to say goodbye. From that moment, with all the energy that his 'steel trap' mind could muster, he made a commitment to Nora...a commitment which never faltered.

Leeroy and Peter's re-publication of their father's book - *A Spy Called Swallow*, is very much a dedication to John - a singular man who was the best possible father his children could ever ask for. A man who always stood by his family, despite enduring years of personal struggles, poverty and grief. During his lifetime he experienced the deaths of his younger sister Irene, and of his two younger brothers, Dimitri and Nicholas. Later, he suffered the death of his wife and the untimely death of his eldest son, also called John. Never complaining, John carried on, as the principled, determined and unbreakable man he was.

PROLOGUE

Like most people, John was imbued with the influences of the age in which he lived. He also possessed the compassion and understanding which resulted from having émigré parents - an Irish mother who departed the shores of the Emerald Isle, fleeing the attentions of the authorities for sympathies contrary to British interests, and a father who was an economic migrant from the Greek island of Kythnos.

Born in Blackpool in 1908, John was well-read by the age of fourteen. He enjoyed books by Rudyard Kipling, Charles Dickens and H.G. Wells who were popular authors at that time and who extolled the virtues of the Great British Empire.

Reading aroused within him a proud sense of his British identity. He desperately wanted to play a part in protecting this identity, if not actively advancing it.

As John's book illustrates, he involved himself in the commerce of the Baltic States. This inevitably brought him into contact with other expats whose sole-purpose was the protection of the Empire at a time of paradigm shifts in political influences, notably the clash between Communism and Nazism.

During the 1930s, countries that had been shackled to the interests of Tsarist Russia began to assert their own nationalistic agendas. They also became subject to the persuasions of other powerful countries trying to break Russia's hold on its former satellites. As John became involved in those fields of operation, he soon came to the attention of various parties and organs-of-state seeking to spread their tentacles. He would have been approached under his commercial guise to perhaps carry 'certain packages', meet 'somebody or other' to make approaches on their behalf for the 'acquisition of products or information'. This was of course all very low key and discrete, but there is no doubt that his various dealings contributed to him being recognised as a player in the game.

No matter what John was called upon to do, he had to be discreet and unassuming, exactly the traits at which he excelled. Years later, his three growing children would delight in his elaborate bedtime stories. Delving into the depths of his infinitely imaginative mind, he would leave them begging for more before the lights finally went out. Sometimes in telling a tale he would stop or hesitate and then mumble something about an 'Official Secrets Act,' which would then be incorporated into the story. Years later, when a job in Holloway Prison for women also necessitated such a declaration of secrecy, he intimated that he was no stranger to such documents.

There's no doubt that secrecy played a big part in his life, and in the lives of so many individuals both before and after the events detailed in his accounts of these torrid times. Working for obscure government organisations, for determined and demanding individuals, keeping secrets would be germane to their very survival and would place them at the epicentre of history as it unfolded.

John disclosed very little to his family about his own involvements. You only have to read between the lines of his book to realise he would have known a great deal about what was going on. It was not his business to question. He simply followed the orders he was given. The one and only occasion he acted independently would be the very time he engaged in another person's secret, a secret so dangerous it could cost him his life. This was Nora's secret, and could have condemned him to terrible tortures, if not death.

The opening sentence of John's article: *How Moscow Recruits Traitors*, written for the news agency Reuters in 1949 states, 'But for my faith and trust in God and love of the land in which I was born, I too, might have been forced to be a traitor.' His book, *A Spy Called Swallow*, published 30 years later is witness to his strongly held beliefs.

During the last few months of John's stay in Moscow he became seriously ill and almost died. The cause of his illness was never really explained, leaving one suspicious about the exact circumstances. What is known, is that it was only through Nora's care and devotion that John recovered and regained his health. Ultimately though, his subsequent poor health was the reason he was sent back to the Home Establishment in the UK – and possibly out of reach of Russian agents.

6

The roles played by Sir Stafford Cripps and Sir Noel-Mason MacFarlane in assisting John and Nora to escape Russia as a married couple must not be underestimated. Mixed marriages between Soviet and British citizens were rarely tolerated at this time. Yet incredibly, permission for their union, along with approval for them to leave Russia was granted by special decree from the leadership of Russia's Central Committee. This fact is all the more remarkable when one considers that this ruling happened during the turmoil and chaos of Germany's invasion of Russia. In fact, they were probably the only British and Russian couple able to leave during the war years, and for some years after.

List of Illustrations

(between pages 96 and 97)

Introduction

Espionage is a word that invariably excites the imagination of all who come across it, and rightly so, for the stakes are high and the pay-off in many cases, death.

If there is any truth in the axiom 'All's fair in love and war', the same may be applied to my own axiom 'There's no game like the spy game', by which I mean that the most innocent and unsuspecting of people are considered 'fair game' for recruitment by those who conduct the business of espionage. Whether these are recruited or coerced into the spy game, there is one thing that sets them apart from the dedicated professional spy. They tend to follow their emotional instincts rather than professional rules, and as such in spite of all the careful selection and examination into their character and background, confound their selectors by acting contrary to all expectations. The experiences and incidents I am about to relate will bear out this assumption.

To give you some idea of my background, I will briefly outline my history: I was born in Blackpool on 7 January 1908, the eldest son among the four children in our family. My younger brothers, Nicholas and Demetri and sister Irene were also born in Lancashire. My father was Greek, and came from Kythnos, one of the small islands near Pireus, and our family name was Varicopulos. My mother was English of Irish descent and was born in Eccles, her maiden name being Murray. We boys all adopted our mother's maiden name which we found much more convenient to use. My father who had arrived in England during his early teens, refused all invitations to take out naturalisation papers averring that he was a true Greek and proud of his ancestry. This decision was apt to cause many difficulties when my parents left England, whereas we children with our British passports experienced no trouble whatsoever when travelling abroad.

After the First World War we moved down to London. It was from there in 1925, aged seventeen, I sailed from Hays Wharf on a cargo boat to Riga, capital city of the then newly-formed Republic of Latvia, to take up an appointment as book-keeper to a Greek cigarette manufacturer. The owner of the factory, a Greek tobacco merchant called Mr Asimakis – an old family friend – had paid my fees for a two-year commercial course at Pitman's College which I attended after leaving St Mark's Preparatory School in Fulham. It was a period when England was in the throes of an economic recession that spelt unemployment and misery to millions. At seventeen, I was in good health and being of an adventurous disposition was prepared to tackle anything; besides I also felt that I owed my benefactor something in return for his kindness.

I arrived in Riga at the end of May 1925 and soon made myself indispensable in the years that followed. In 1927 I went to Kovno, the capital of the neighbouring republic of Lithuania, and assisted my employer in the opening of another cigarette factory. It was during my sojourn in Lithuania that I made the acquaintance of a young army lieutenant called Alexsis Balunas, who was an aide to the Minister of Defence. His English was very poor and in the course of our friendship I wrote many letters on his behalf ordering armaments required by Lithuania from the well-known British firm of Armstrong Vickers.

In 1931, my employer suddenly died intestate and his relatives started litigation proceedings over his estate. Legal costs practically brought the factories to a state of bankruptcy and the Riga firm was closed down. The family differences were finally settled in 1932 and I was able to sell the Kovno factory for them. The commission I earned enabled me to leave Lithuania and buy up the factory in Riga which I re-opened. I brought my father and mother, together with my brother Nicholas, to Riga and set about building up the business anew. I was soon employing a work force of over three hundred, and we became one of the largest cigarette factories in Latvia.

It was in Riga that I made the acquaintance of a Latvian ex-airforce pilot who designed and built his own aeroplanes. He knew no English so I undertook his correspondence with Bristol for the purchase of Gypsy aero engines which were the only ones he would use. This association, like that with Lieutenant Balunas, was later to have far-reaching consequences. I was completely unaware at the time that Soviet spies operating in Lithuania and Latvia had reported these connections to Soviet Intelligence who promptly put me on their list for future attention.

In 1937 my factory was nationalised together with other British firms by the Latvian government. It came as a shock, the compensation paid was hardly sufficient to cover the cost of the machinery and to make matters worse I could not even take this money out of the country owing to currency restrictions. Furthermore, to make things even more difficult I had my personal employment and residential permits cancelled. My father and brother were asked to remain as consultants to the tobacco industry. As my parents had grown to like Riga and had made many friends there they agreed to remain, but my brother after only a short period returned to London.

I then decided to go to Helsinki in Finland where I had several business acquaintances. I had two reasons for doing this. First it was near enough for me to keep an eye on the welfare of my parents, and secondly I wanted to be near at hand so that, should developments permit it, I would be able to get my money out of Latvia and procure a further indemnity for the loss of the factory. In this I failed, I was never again to see my money or get proper compensation for my factory.

I was not to know this. Nor was I to know that my decision to go to Finland was to result in my being enrolled as a diplomatic courier, and in my travels I was to eye-witness the invasion and annexation by the Germans and the Soviets of one country after another. That I was to escape capture and death by the skin of my teeth. That I was to get involved with a beautiful Russian spy who ended my bachelor days by embarking on a perilous three-month voyage in an Arctic convoy as my Soviet bride. Such is Fate.

Part I

War comes to Finland

Arriving in Finland in the September of 1937 meant starting all over again right from the bottom. But it was not long before I got a job with a Finnish firm of exporters and importers dealing mainly in timber and textiles. The state of the world economy was still very bad and trade suffered from currency restrictions imposed by various European countries endeavouring to maintain their balance of foreign commitments. To offset this my firm transacted business under a barter system that was both unique and interesting and I soon became quite adept at arranging exports of Finnish goods to the Levant and Germany in exchange for consumer goods required by Finland. The director of the firm I worked for was a very distinguished gentleman known as Consul Arvi Paloheimo whose wife was the daughter of Jean Sibelius, the great Finnish composer.

All in all I loved Finland. It was a beautiful country, its forests and innumerable lakes whether in summer or winter held a peculiar fascination for me. It was a country of natural brooding loveliness. The long drawn-out winters with their intensive dry cold weather were similar to those I had experienced in other Baltic States and it suited my temperament.

I made many friends and found that in business they were the most straightforward people I had ever dealt with. I was kept so busy that the first year in Finland passed unnoticed. Politically, I was well aware of what was going on in Europe but it seemed so far away and Finland such a haven of peace, that it was the best place to be in.

During the summer of 1939 I felt particularly honoured to receive a personal invitation to attend the birthday party of Jean

Sibelius. Here I must mention that I had written several letters for him in English replying to the many demands he received from the great orchestras in England and America to conduct performances of his works. Although still vigorous, he was reluctant to leave his native country, apart from which he was still occupied on important compositions.

The party was quite a magnificent affair and took place in the gardens of the Paloheimo estate. The set tables gleamed and glittered with a fantastic array of silver and crystalware. There were about two hundred guests and besides all the Finnish notables there were members from almost every foreign diplomatic legation resident in Helsinki. The festivities ended with a splendid fireworks display, a treat that his grandchildren had arranged as a surprise for him. There were so many toasts drunk that I'm afraid that I don't know how I got home that night.

It was not long after this party, 1 September 1939 to be exact, that the whole world was stunned by the news of the German invasion of Poland. Alarmed by what might happen should the conflagration spread to Latvia, which after all was not far from Poland, I left the next day by plane for Riga to join my mother and father and it was on the following day, 3 September, we sat huddled together listening to the radio broadcast announcing Britain's ultimatum to Germany. We looked at one another in stunned silence as the news came through. Finally my mother remarked,

'Well that's it! Let's have a cup of tea.'

I remained with my parents till the end of the month reassuring them that all would be well and not to worry. Life in Riga seemed on the surface to be still running smoothly and my father was quite happy carrying on with his work there – which made things easier. It was during this period I received a letter from my firm enclosing a sealed envelope from the British Consulate in Helsinki. It contained brief instructions from Mr Waite, the Consul, to report immediately to the British Military Attaché in Helsinki and added that it was a decree applicable to all British subjects of military age living abroad. I did not mention the letter to my parents.

I went to the Legation as soon as I arrived in Helsinki and on presenting myself was greeted with the laconic remark,

'I don't think we will send you home Murray, you'll be a lot more use to us this side of the world.'

The interview ended with my being told to stand by for further instructions which would be sent to me in due course.

I returned home that evening bewildered and isolated and spent the time thinking things over. What were my thoughts at the time? All I can remember was the bitterness I felt. Three times since leaving England I had striven to build up a life that would afford some degree of independence and security only to see my efforts come to nought. Now there was a war to be reckoned with. What my part in it was to be I had not the faintest idea. I remembered my uncles Costa and George, both Greek, who had fought with the British forces in the First World War; my cousins on my mother's side, Harold who had come home badly wounded with a gaping hole in his side, and Roland the ever-smiling boy who had gone to the front when only seventeen and had never returned. How my mother had cried when she received the news of his death. They had all been my boyhood heroes, but it all seemed so far removed from what was happening now.

I had learned a lot since leaving England, especially about the Nazis with whom I had come into contact through the Balt Germans. I knew much of the fallacies of communism through my own workers in Kovno and Riga and was well aware of the existence of underground hard-core cells on both sides of the political spectrum throughout the Baltic States. I was never a talker, but always a good listener. Both creeds to me were obnoxious. During the latter years the looming clouds of war had given rise to a general consensus of opinion among our people in the Baltic that war was inevitable, but it would be between the Fascists and the Communists whilst we would sit on the fence and watch them destroy one another. The non-aggression pact however, signed between Germany and the Soviets had now upset the scheme of things and I realised only too well the danger that threatened Britain. As far as I was concerned there was no doubt in which direction my duty lay and having arrived at this conclusion I decided to give up worrying and let the future take care of itself.

At about 9 a.m. on the morning of 30 November 1939, I was sitting deep in thought in a café in Helsinki, having a coffee prior to going to the office, when I suddenly looked up to see the place completely empty. Further, a Finnish soldier carrying a rifle was banging on the window gesticulating to me to leave the place. I got up hurriedly. He grabbed me by the arm and seeing I was a foreigner, kept shouting 'Russky, Russky!' and pointed to the sky. I heard guns booming in the distance and looking up saw scattered puffs of smoke appearing high in the cloudless deep blue sky, with planes glinting silvery in the morning light. I decided that I would go to the nearby flat of one of my friends Fred Bucknall and warn him of what was happening. I arrived at his flat which was on the third floor of the building and found him calmly shaving in the bathroom. 'Have you heard the news?' I cried. 'Yes, it's all right, it's only the Russky's bombing Helsinki!' he said. 'What are we going to do now?' I asked, not having a clue what to do, everything had happened so suddenly.

'I shall go to the office and then on to the bank to see if I can draw some money, if you can take the wife and the kiddy down to the cellar while this is on John, I'd be very grateful. I'll try and get back as quickly as possible.'

His wife and little girl came down with me to the cellar. I emptied a basin of lump sugar into my pockets as we went. The large cellar was crowded with men, women and children and I noticed that it had been hastily shorn up with huge baulks of raw timber. So the Finns had been expecting something like this I thought, and here was me, as ignorant as a coot of what had been happening around me! And I thought I knew everything. I was glad I'd taken the sugar lumps. We could hear the boom of bombs as they exploded mingling with the quick sharp continuous reports of the anti-aircraft guns. All this set the children crying. I went around giving them sugar lumps, laughing and talking to them. It had a good effect. After a couple of hours, the all-clear was given. Fred returned and I decided to make my way to my own office. On the way I had to go past the coffee house. It was a shambles – no windows, and all the tables turned over and chairs in a jumble. The street itself was ankle deep in jagged pieces of broken glass. Before the café lay a tram on its side, a mass of twisted iron as though some giant hand had crumpled it up.

When I arrived at the office no one was there so I returned to my rooms, still wondering what to do next. The next day I went to the office again. This time Dagni, one of the clerks was there. From her I gathered the details of the Russian attack of Finland. Mr Paloheimo had, as yet, not been to the office and she did not know when he would come. The bottom of the world had seemingly fallen out. I decided to go to the Legation. On the way there another raid started. A bomb must have fallen somewhere down the end of the road. I didn't hear anything but all of a sudden, a terrific blast of air lifted me off my feet and I was hurled backwards over quite a distance. Stunned, with my head buzzing, fit to burst, I got to my feet. I felt drunk. Many years afterwards during an Army medical I was told the scars on my ear drums were probably due to blast perforation.

I continued on my way to the British Legation and saw Mr Desmond, the Chancellery servant who I knew quite well. He told me the Legation staff were preparing to leave for a safer place somewhere on the coast. He had to remain as they had to have someone in the building to attend to the postal and telegraph communications that would still be coming in. He said that feeling lonely he would feel happier if I could join him. He had got a fairly good shelter in the basement so I stayed with him, giving him what assistance I could. The days passed with alarms and raids to enliven our existence. All I knew was that the Finns were putting up a good fight, which knowing them, was only what I expected, though I could not see much hope of them winning.

On the afternoon of 4 December 1939, Mr Bamford, the British Vice-Consul suddenly appeared in the Legation and informed me that most of the British Colony was to be evacuated to Stockholm in Sweden and would leave Helsingfors that very night. It was an urgent and imperative order and my name was on the list. I was to report to the British Consul at 7 p.m. that evening. I went to the Consulate at seven and found about forty people assembled. Among them was Mr Beck, Reuter's Finnish correspondent. We more or less teamed up together. I had no luggage, as there had been no time to collect anything. All I had was the black leather briefcase with my personal documents, passport, etc., that I always carried with me. Apart from a few socks, pants and vests I had stuffed into it, there was a little statuette of the Madonna that travelled everywhere I went. I had brought this along to the Legation as a kind of mascot, a gesture that Mr Desmond being a Catholic, warmly appreciated.

Bamford was in charge, and soon we found ourselves on the train for Turku, the Finnish west coast port where we were to embark for Stockholm. We had been travelling for about two and a half hours when the train stopped. The sliding door at the end of the coach opened and in strode half a dozen fully armed Finnish soldiers. Their faces were grim as they walked down the centre of the coach peering intently at the occupants on either side as they passed. As they came to Bamford, who was seated in the middle section, one of the soldiers grabbed him roughly and hauled him to his feet, shouting angrily in Finnish. Poor Bamford looked startled and was not even given a chance to speak as they tried to drag him along.

Beck who knew Finnish fairly well said to me, 'Crikey, they think he is a Russian spy.' We both jumped up and I went forward waving my British passport in the soldiers' faces, shouting 'Leave him alone, he's our British Consul, we are all English here!' Just then an officer appeared and seeing the struggle that was going on gave a sharp order and the soldiers let Bamford go. Then a whole series of explanations followed with Bamford producing his documents. An apology was made and thankfully accepted. It appeared that the Finns had information that a Russian spy or spies had boarded the train. Bamford, who wore a fur cap and long black coat, had aroused their suspicions. We arrived in Turku, which was still burning from an air-raid, just after midnight. Through the rubble we were quickly shepherded to a small Finnish steam packet that had just arrived in the harbour. We sailed almost immediately. Even the upper decks were crowded with refugees. It was one of the most bitterly cold sea voyages I have ever made.

We arrived in Stockholm in the early hours of 5 December. As the ship approached Stockholm, we saw the city with all its lights full on, such a contrast to Helsingfors where a black-out had been enforced. When we docked, all passengers except the British were disembarked. A British Consular official came aboard later and our papers and passports were checked against a list. Beck, some others and myself, were then driven to a small private hotel where some of the lesser Embassy staff lived, and given private rooms with instructions to report to the Embassy later in the day. I remember asking Beck why the evacuation had been so sudden, reckoning that he, as a newspaper man would know something, because we had been given no information at all. He said that a rumour had been circulating that the Russians were going to use poison gas on Helsingfors, which of course they never did.

At the first opportunity I wrote to my parents in Latvia, to let them know I was safe in Sweden and if possible to contact Glynn Hall, the British Vice-Consul in Riga, and get him to transfer some money over to me. Very shortly I received one hundred pounds through the Embassy with a letter from my mother saying they were well and I was to look after myself and not to get into trouble.

Although we had breakfast at our hotel, our main midday meals were taken together with other members of the Embassy at a large restaurant in the centre of the city. It was quite amusing; we used to occupy a couple of large tables, next to us would be a Japanese contingent on one side, and on the other, several tables with German Legation staff. We used to sit down pointedly ignoring them. Sometimes our chaps would draw our attention to several ordinary looking fellows sitting apart whom they whispered were foreign secret agents known to them.

It appeared that quite a number of German secret service agents were operating in Stockholm under the guise of businessmen. I was not surprised at this information, because I had come across similar types in Lithuania and Latvia. They had appeared in the Baltic States shortly after Hitler had assumed power in Germany. They were, in fact, mostly ex-army officers from the First World War and their job was to recruit young Baltic Germans for the Hitler Youth Brigades. How I came to know this was that my brother and I had formerly been members of KSK – a Baltic-German Sports Club – he played football for them and I boxed in the club. As we both spoke German we got to hear about these special visitors from Germany.

I found Stockholm a beautiful and interesting city with many imposing buildings, especially the large royal palace set on the crown of a hill. Waterways seemed to run in and all round the city. Whilst I was there, the newly built Princess Charlotta hospital was opened for public inspection. I went to see it and was very impressed indeed with its lay-out and up-to-date chromium and nickel-plated equipment and the bright silent flooring and sliding doors. I should imagine that at that time it must have been the finest hospital in Europe.

Beck was very restless in Sweden and confided to me that Reuters had been expecting him to station himself on the Finnish front, which for various reasons he had been reluctant to do. His wife who was Finnish had not come with him and his son, although only eighteen, had gone off to volunteer for service with the Finnish Army. His father could not stop him – such is youth! A famous reporter by the name of Walter Durante had arrived in Stockholm, representing World Press News and Beck invited me to go along with him to see the great man who was well known to him. I think he was staying at the Grand Hotel. It was about ten in the morning, and Walter was lying on a large double bed in his pyjamas. The bed was littered with a number of Swedish newspapers. On either side of the bed sat a couple of the most beautiful blonde Swedish girls I had ever seen. There were also a couple of cases of bottled beer. Walter, after introductions, waved with one glass of beer in his hand and the other holding a newspaper, for us to be seated and help ourselves which we did. I followed the subsequent proceedings with some amusement. Walter would point to a caption under a picture in the newspaper and one of the blondes would translate it into English. Thereupon, he would dictate a telegram message for the other blonde to take down and after several such, she would go off to despatch them. His dictation ran as follows:

'From our special correspondent on the Finnish front stop Temperature now 40° below zero stop Under appalling conditions saw . . .'

and then would follow rehashed texts in journalese from the Swedish newspapers. Beck was quite aggrieved by all this, as Reuters were now using Durante's services. It was a bit of an eye-opener to me, but it did not alter the fact that Walter Durante was nevertheless a great man in the profession as I came to know later. He was a newshound who would go anywhere and was just as tenacious as a bulldog.

Reporting in at the Embassy one day in February 1940, I was summoned to the Chargé d'Affaire's office and told I was to prepare myself for a trip to Oslo as a diplomatic courier. On 9 February 1940, the first secretary handed me an envelope about five inches square, heavily sealed at all corners and the centre, addressed to the British Minister, Sir Cecil Dormer at Oslo. After signing several 'Official Secret' declarations I was told it was to be handed to Sir Cecil personally. I was to guard it with my life etc., etc., I cockily replied that they could safely leave me to carry out the instructions given. The Secretary asked me how I was going to carry the envelope. I opened my jacket, then my waistcoat showing that inside the lining of my waistcoat were two pockets. I had always had my tailors make such pockets which I used for carrying either large sums of money or confidential documents. He nodded his head satisfied. Then he said I was to see the Chancellery servant and get my tickets and reservation forms and leave that night on the midnight express. I had to hang about in the Embassy until it was time to leave. Just before eleven I got my papers. I had no luggage, only the old black leather briefcase filled as before.

Now there were two Chancellery servants in the Embassy, a father and son. The father was the senior and had served the Embassy many years with distinction and had been awarded the OBE for his services. His son was a tall, lanky fellow, always smiling and affable, but too effusive for my liking. The older man, white-haired and portly, was always quite serious in his manner. This night it was the younger man on duty, and the Embassy at this hour seemed practically deserted. I asked him particulars about the trip I was to make, as the journey from Stockholm to Oslo was new to me. I particularly wanted to know the length and time the journey would take and the border station at which I must expect passport and customs control. I had travelled much in Europe, and I knew that this was important to anyone going from one country to another. While he was explaining, he opened the drawer of his desk and took out a big black German Mauser automatic revolver and handed it to me.

'You'll want one of these for your journey.' I handled it gingerly. I had never possessed or fired a revolver in my life.

'Is it loaded?' I asked, trying to look as though handling revolvers was all in a day's work. He took it off me – 'Yes, but the safety catch is on, so it's all right now,' and he pointed it at the passage wall where some coats were hanging. He must have squeezed the trigger as he pointed, because flames suddenly shot out of the muzzle and five shots rattled out one after the other but so quickly, that it sounded like one. He was so shocked he dropped the gun, and people came running into the passage from all directions. There was one hell of a hubbub over the damaged clothes. In the midst of the row that followed I looked at my watch. I had not much time, so I slipped out, caught a taxi to the station, found my train and reserved compartment and settled down. All these events were to be very important to me, though I did not know it at the time. Many years after the war had ended this young Chancellery servant brought disgrace on his father's name by being found out and convicted whilst still in the employ of our Embassy as a spy in the pay of the Russians. Whether he was a spy for the Germans at the time I was in the Embassy, I do not know.

As I settled down in my compartment I recalled the fate of two other diplomatic couriers. One whose mutilated body had been found on the railway lines, verdict – sad case of falling out of a moving train whilst under the influence of alcohol. The other, whose newspaper photo depicted him sprawled half out of his bunk in a sleeping-car with a knife stuck between his ribs, verdict – suicide whilst of unsound mind. In both cases the diplomatic documents they were carrying were missing and the incidents hushed up to avoid political embarrassment. Musing on these events, I got up and made a quick survey of the first class coach to see who my fellow travellers might be. The coach was empty, I would be travelling alone. The reason was that all the sensible travellers had booked warm cosy sleepers. It was mid-winter and a very cold one at that. I locked the sliding door to my compartment and taking off my overcoat, huddled into a corner and was soon into a kind of half-doze, not daring to sleep. How many hours went by I do not know, when suddenly I became aware of a dark figure looming against the glass of the door, there was a rattle of the lock being turned from the outside, a click, and in stepped what seemed to be a mountain of a man. He had no hat, no coat, no luggage. He closed the door and sat directly opposite me, his knees almost touching mine. I was startled. That door had been locked, only a conductor with a master key could open it from the outside. This man was no conductor. From under half-closed eyes I looked him over. I had made no movement and remained as I was when he came in. I was frightened, I had reason to be. He was a bull of a man, his bulk dominating the compartment. The pair of huge hands with the thick powerful fingers resting on his knees filled me with a kind of fascinated horror. One of those huge hands around my neck and it would snap like a matchstick. I could not help shuddering at the thought.

That he was a foreign agent I had not the slightest doubt. He looked like a German to me and I was doubly alarmed. From under a closely-cropped bullet head, a pair of watery-blue piggy eyes surveyed me with studied calculation and then wandered speculatively to the black leather briefcase at my side and the over-coat I had carelessly flung beside it. The maker's name, Elias Jakobson of Riga, on the ornate label showing very prominently. Questions were tumbling through my mind at an incredible rate. Who was the fellow? Did he know I was a courier? If so, how had he got the information? And, if he attacked me, what could I do? The slightest move on my part might start him off. I knew I didn't stand a cat in hell's chance against a chap like this. I tensed inwardly, watching him for any sudden movement. I noticed his eyes slightly narrowing as though he was doing some thinking. Evidently he was not quite satisfied about something. The Jewish name on the label of my overcoat seemed to draw his attention. It occurred to me that he might have been tipped off that a courier would be travelling on the train, but did not know for certain his identity. I had often been mistaken for a Jew with my dark curly hair and longish nose and I wondered if he thought I was one. All of a sudden my thoughts were interrupted by his addressing me with a guttural 'Good evening!' in English. I looked at him blankly. He spoke again.

'I said "Good evening!" Is it not?'

I shrugged my shoulders and spread my hands out deprecatingly, 'I do not understand what you want of me, I don't understand anything!' I replied in my best German-Yiddish manner.

'*Pfui!*' He spat dramatically on the floor of the compartment in disgust.

'*Noch eine verdammte Jude!*' (Another damned Jew.)

And he nodded his head to add emphasis to the words. As for me I had a sudden feeling of relief, blessing the time I had spent many years previously with a Jewish family called Levinson in order to learn German. They taught me Yiddish. Only later when I proudly attempted to air my newly-acquired knowledge with a Balt German called Schwedrup Schwedler, the head book-keeper of the factory I worked in, was I to learn my mistake. He had acted in exactly the same manner.

This sudden change in the situation undoubtedly saved my life as well as the despatch I carried. But I was still worried about the fix I was in, and I could feel the German was not yet sure of his ground. In an altered tone he asked me if I'd ever been in Germany. I told him yes, and mentioned the towns I had visited in the course of business, then I added plaintively that it was a pity the Germans had such a hatred for the Jews, whereupon he went off into a long tirade about the Jews ruining Germany by making money and illegally taking it out of the country, so harming the financial state of Germany. All the time he was talking I was calculating in my mind how soon we would reach the Norwegian border because I knew the passport and custom control officers would appear and it would give me the chance of doing something about the plight I was in.

During a brief interlude in our conversation when I thought the time was ripe I stood up, not even bothering to glance at my briefcase or coat and asked him at which end of the coach the toilets were. He did not know, so excusing myself, I slid the door back and went into the corridor to find them myself. He did not make any attempt to stop me, and I breathed a silent prayer as I went out. Reaching the toilets, I hastily locked the door and with my back to the wall stretched out my right leg to jam the door. I was lucky. Not long afterwards, though it seemed ages to me, the train slowed down and then stopped. Within a few minutes I heard the trampling of heavy boots and my door was tried, then banged upon and a shout bade me open for passport control. I opened the door and five large uniformed officers stood outside. Quickly I showed my passport and courier documents and explained that a German had made an unwarranted entry into my compartment. Without a word they all turned, and went down the corridor to my compartment. I remained where I was. I heard a lot of shouting and banging going on, and shortly afterwards, the officers returned and led me to my compartment, saying, 'Don't worry, you won't be disturbed any more!' When they had gone, I examined my briefcase – it had been wrenched open and the lock was broken.

The rest of the journey passed without incident but I felt terribly relieved when the train steamed into Oslo station. I waited in my compartment until a young man appeared who asked me if I was Mr Murray from the Embassy in Stockholm. He introduced himself and said he was from the Legation in Oslo where he then took me and introduced me to the First Secretary, Mr Lascelles, and to the Minister, Sir Cecil Dormer, to whom I gave the sealed envelope I had been carrying. On being asked if I'd had a pleasant trip, I recounted my experience on the train. Sir Cecil was quite upset, especially over the fact that I had been unaccompanied by an Embassy official to the station in Stockholm. He said it was a breach of the regulations and would send off a complaint immediately to Stockholm. He then asked me to wait whilst they both went into the Minister's private study. I waited thinking that I would be instructed to go on another assignment. After some minutes, Mr Lascelles returned and asked me if I would consider staying on in the Legation in the capacity of night security guard. He explained that they formerly had three, working in alternate shifts, but one of them had met with an unfortunate skiing accident and was in hospital with a broken leg and the Legation urgently needed a temporary replacement and they would be very grateful if I would consider the matter. I did not hesitate and told him I would accept the post and carry on as long as it would be necessary. I signed another set of official secrecy forms and was then introduced to my opposite number, Mr Gobby, an ex-naval marine with whom I was to share quarters at a private hotel in Oslo.

All I remember about Oslo was that it was a quiet peaceful city. The people were very friendly and kind. There was such an air of calm and a total absence of uniformed soldiers such as I'd been accustomed to see in Germany and the Baltic States, that it almost seemed that I was back in England. The news coming through about the war was not bad. The Navy was keeping the Germans penned in and our troops in France were keeping such a formidable check on the Germans that it seemed the whole business of war might peter out. Such was the general feeling, but all too soon events were to prove us wrong.

Part II

War comes to Norway

On the evening of 8 April 1940, I arrived for duty at the Legation some few minutes before six, to find several of the staff only just beginning to lock away their papers prior to going home. Normally they were already away by the time I took over from the day officer. It had evidently been a day of quite exceptional activity. By eight o'clock the building was empty except for the Minister who was still in his office adjoining the library. In any case, this was not unusual as his official residence was on the top floor of the building. On arrival I had switched over the telephones at the reception desk, checked my requirements for the night: torch, candles, recording clock, and the handy iron bar which I thought could be useful in an emergency – and watched the remaining staff leave. The last to go were the Naval Attaché and the First Secretary. As soon as they had gone I commenced my rounds of the building, checking all doors and windows and recording on my clock the various key points.

My check times took place at hourly intervals and I'd often wished something would happen to break the deadly monotony of these nightly vigils. Beyond a few phone calls and the occasional appearance of Mr Lascelles for spot checks to see everything was in order, nothing ever happened. It was just after ten when the library door opened and Sir Cecil came out.

'Good evening Murray. Everything all right?'

'All's well,' I answered, and added, 'but you seem to be having a long day of it today, Sir.'

He stroked his chin and nodded.

'Yes, I'm afraid it has been a heavy day.' He sighed and continued, 'I am very tired, Murray, and am going to turn in. Will you please tell any callers that I am not to be disturbed under any circumstances. If you should be in doubt, put the call through to my butler.'

'Very good, Sir. I'll see to it,' I said.

As he turned to go, he added, 'Oh, and by the way, there's a plate of sandwiches in the library. I've told the butler to leave them for you.' He was always very informal and it was such gestures that made working for him a real pleasure. I thanked him and with a final goodnight he went off, little knowing how soon his plans for a good night's sleep were to be shattered. The hours passed slowly by: no calls, no interruptions. It looked like being another uneventful night. At about two o'clock I got up to make another round of inspection and had just reached the end of the corridor when all the lights began to flicker and suddenly went out. I switched my torch on and rushed back to the desk. The sudden change from light to blackness did not unduly perturb me. I put it down to a power failure, especially as glancing through the windows I noticed there was total darkness outside.

I rummaged through the drawers of the desk and found a couple of candles, lit them, and stuck them on the desk. I had no sooner done so and was wondering what to do next, when a series of heavy booms broke the darkened silence. Gunfire! No mistaking the sound. I'd heard it only too often in Finland. But they did not continue. I got up to look through one of the windows – it was still black outside and once again all was silence. Still undecided about what to do, I returned to my desk and a gradual feeling of apprehension began to overtake me. I had the feeling once again that things had been too good to last. Something was about to happen. What it was, I didn't know, but in any case my job was to hang on until there was some definite directive as to my next course of action. The Minister had given me strict instructions he was not to be disturbed and in any case, all was silent now, only the lights weren't working. The sudden ringing of the telephone bell seemed like an explosion in itself. I grabbed the receiver – 'The British Legation here. Who is it please?'

A thick precise voice preceded by audible heavy breathing answered me. 'Please, I must speak with the Minister, it is very urgent!'

'I'm afraid I can't get the Minister for you, he has retired for the night and I have strict instructions not to disturb him, but, who is that speaking, and can I take a message?'

'But please, I MUST speak to him. This is the Prime Minister of Norway speaking. The Germans are invading my country now! Please, I must speak to your Minister!'

'Hold the line Your Excellency, I'll get him for you immediately,' I replied, ringing through at the same time to the Minister's apartment. Within a few seconds the sleepy voice of the Minister's butler came through, 'What do you want?' he demanded.

'Get Sir Cecil on the line immediately . . .' as he was about to protest I added, 'I've got the Prime Minister of Norway on the phone, it's extremely urgent.'

Within seconds Sir Cecil came on the line. 'Well, Murray, what is it?'

'It's the Prime Minister of Norway, Sir. He says the Germans are invading his country. I'm switching you through now, Sir.'

I heard a muttered 'Good God' as I switched the line over.

That is how the first news of the invasion of Norway by the Germans was given to our Minister, Sir Cecil Dormer, by the Norwegian Prime Minister, Johan Nygaarsvold.

A few minutes later, there was a click on the switchboard denoting the end of the call and shortly after that I heard the door of the library at the end of the corridor open, and Sir Cecil appeared holding a lighted candle above his head. He was wearing a dressing gown over his pyjamas. He hurried towards me. 'Oh, there you are, Murray. Good. Now listen to me. You know what it's all about. I want you to ring up as many of the staff as you can get hold of as quickly as you can. Tell them to come to the Legation immediately, bringing what valuables they can with them and tell them not to waste any time. Those are my orders! Should they ask any questions, you are not to mention the invasion, just make it plain that they are my personal instructions. I am going to get dressed now, and will be down very shortly. In the meantime, do your very best; we have very little time.'

One by one I got the Service Attachés and the Secretaries, and then the others of the staff. The first to arrive was Mr Lascelles who was already aware of the situation. He gave me an approving nod and hurried to the Minister's rooms. Some of the staff were quick to realise that the call was urgent beyond question; others began to hum and haw, but when I informed them that they were holding things up as I had to contact all the staff, they realised that something really serious was afoot. The Senior Chancellery Servant arrived, and when I mentioned the news, he was visibly shocked – his wife was Norwegian and he had only recently set up home just outside Oslo. He now took over the telephone, whilst I gave a hand in the frenetic activity of destroying all documents likely to be of use to the enemy. The order had been given out that the Legation was to be evacuated immediately, and already part of the staff were busily engaged in loading every available car. Meanwhile the lights had suddenly come on again, which greatly facilitated our activities. By now, of course, everyone knew that Norway was being invaded by German troops. What they did not know, was whether any resistance was being put up by the Norwegians and what was more important, how much time there was left to get out before the enemy arrived on the scene.

In spite of the seeming confusion, everything went as methodically and as smoothly as circumstances permitted. By about three-thirty a.m. on 10 April a convoy of cars began to stream out of the Legation grounds into the deserted road. A notable feature was the arrival of the head of the American Legation, a woman, whose car roof was adorned with a huge American flag, its stars and stripes distinctly visible and covering the whole top of the car. I guessed it was for possible protection from air attack and some sort of protection for the convoy itself, the United States still being a neutral country at that time. It seemed very odd to me that a woman should be holding such a high diplomatic post, but I could not help admiring her courage in undertaking the forthcoming journey with its unknown hazards.

There were now only three of us left – the Senior Chancellery Servant, Jack, Ted, the day security officer, and myself. As we stood silently watching the cars move off, the last one stopped and Mr Lascelles, the Chargé d'Affaires, got out and came over to give us our final instructions. These were to await the arrival of members of the American Legation who would affix United States seals on the building so it would come under their custody. Meanwhile, we were to complete the destruction of the remaining documents, and then make our way to Narvik, which was over six hundred miles away, and might present some difficulty especially as we hadn't even a car. So I asked him if there was any possibility of getting a car.

'I'm sorry Murray,' he said, 'but we've commandeered every car possible and are already overloaded. We've got to join up with the Norwegian Government who have already headed north. I'm afraid you'll have to do the best you can – at all costs keep out of German hands. Best of luck. We'll be seeing you!'

With that he drove off with the rest. We looked at one another, our thoughts as bleak as the grey morning sky overhead. Of the three, I was the best off: Jack, the Chancellery Servant was married to a Norwegian and Ted, who had a Norwegian fiancée living in Oslo, must have also been thinking about her; whilst I had no ties.

'Come on, let's get cracking,' said Ted, breaking the silence.

With that we started collecting all the remaining papers we could find and dumped them in the garden. With a gallon or so of petrol we soon had quite a fire going. I went off to make a final check on all the rooms and returned to the bonfire.

'Look at those bastards over there,' Jack said, pointing to the building on the opposite side of the road some fifty yards away. It was the German Legation, and every room was lit up, and we could see shadows of figures moving constantly behind the curtained windows.

'I wonder what they're up to,' I said.

'Perhaps they're getting ready to attack us,' said Ted.

'We'll keep away from the fire, we don't want to be sitting targets should they start shooting,' said Jack jokingly.

But nevertheless, we moved into the shadow of the trees. In the distance we could hear the clang of a fire engine approaching; it gradually grew louder and then, to our surprise, we saw the fire engine appear and draw up outside the gates. The firemen on it jumped down and began hammering on the gates which were locked.

'Go on Jack, see what they want. Your Norwegian is better than mine,' I said. He went off and I could see he was doing a lot of gesticulating. At the same time I noticed the shadows behind the curtains opposite were no longer moving but seemed all bunched together. There was no doubt we were under surveillance. After a while the firemen could be seen remounting their engine and they drove off.

Jack returned. 'It's them Jerries,' he said. 'They phoned up the fire brigade and told them we were burning the place down. I told them they'd got it all wrong and that we were only celebrating an old English custom called Guy Fawkes to ward off evil spirits!'

'Blast them Jerries,' said Ted. 'I wish those Americans would hurry up before they arrive.'

He had no sooner spoken than a car drew up. It was the Americans. We let them in and I told Jack to take them round as quickly as he could and get the sealing-up done, in order that we could get away. It had already gone four o'clock and it was getting lighter every minute. Jack shook his head. 'No, you two go on. I'm going to stay. I'll go back to the missus and we'll hole up somewhere in the mountains. You go. I'll see to the Americans.'

I could see the sense of it at the time. There was no use arguing, and if I'd had a wife like him, I would have probably done the same. Ted was also turning things over in his mind too. They'd both lived in the peace and quiet of Norway for so long, that the invasion did not seem real to them. He said his fiancée would be worrying about him and perhaps he'd be safer joining her. I reminded him we had been given definite instructions. As an ex-Grenadier Guard (for he was only on loan from the War Office to the Legation for security duties) his habit of strict discipline was the deciding factor, and he agreed to come with me.

'Come on Ted,' I finally said. 'Let's get going.' We exchanged wishes for the best of luck with Jack and made for the gates. As we were unlocking them to go out, a man came running up the road. He was well-built, clean-shaven, had no hat but wore a blue serge overcoat. He stopped in front of us. 'This is the Legation?' he asked in perfect English. I nodded.

'Take me to the Minister,' he said.

'Who are you?' I asked.

'Look, my name is Williams and I've got to see the Minister,' he said. I then knew who I was talking to. Mr Williams was one of our 'Hush' men. He was, in fact, a Lieutenant Commander in the Royal Navy sent over on a special mission, dressed of course, in ordinary civilian attire. He'd been expected earlier and I had been informed of this possible arrival though no one knew when he would actually turn up. I explained the situation to him and asked him how he had managed to get to the Legation. He told me that on arrival in Oslo the evening before, he was so fagged out that he had put up in a hotel to get a night's sleep, with the intention of calling on the Legation first thing in the morning. About an hour ago he had been awakened by the sound of banging doors and the trampling of heavy feet with a lot of shouting going on.

'I got up,' he said, 'and looked out of the window and saw a crowd of German soldiers in the street. I didn't wait. I got dressed and slipped out, and here I am!'

'It looks as though we had better get moving quick!' I remarked.

Whilst we were talking another figure arrived on the scene. It was the Rev. Linton, Chaplain to the Legation, and on explaining the situation all over again to him, he was most indignant that the staff had gone off without him.

It was a strange situation. None of us had the slightest idea of how we were going to get out of Oslo. One thing was clear, and that was that we had to get out and get out quickly. We talked amongst ourselves and finally decided that the only thing to do would be to start walking and hope for the best. The idea was to reach a railway station and try and get a train going north. Failing that, to make for the airfields and see if we could fly back to England. In the meantime, we'd try and pick up a taxi or a car to get us out of the danger zone.

With this in mind, we called to Jack, who locked the gates behind us – said cheerio to the Americans who'd practically finished their job of sealing the Legation doors, and started to walk down the road leading away from the city.

It was already half-light. The residential area through which we walked was quiet and deserted. We kept to the shadows of the tree-lined roadway. How long we trudged along, silently, each one busy with his own thoughts, I don't know. One seemed to have lost count of time and we didn't even have any idea where the road led to, except that it was leading us away from the city.

Looking back over my shoulder from the way we had come, I saw a car coming. I thought I'd take a chance and try to stop it, so I ran into the road and waved my arms. The car stopped and the driver pulled down the windows as I approached. I could see he was a civilian, and in halting Norwegian I asked him if he could give my friends and I a lift. He smiled and said, 'You are English, aren't you?' I showed him my passport, and seeing that it was unnecessary to struggle along with my imperfect Norwegian, I explained the plight we were in. It was a chance in a million! Within a few seconds we were all in the car and bowling along at top speed away from the capital. He explained that he himself was fleeing from Oslo and was going north to join the Norwegian Army if it was still in existence. He said he'd no doubt the British would be coming to the aid of Norway, and was hoping to fight alongside them. He showed me his Army reserve papers to prove he had been an officer. There was no doubt about his sincerity, and we all had the utmost confidence in his ability to get us out of the scrape we were in. Discussing our plans as we drove along, he said the idea of picking up a train en route would not be feasible as by now, if any trains were running, they would already have been commandeered by the Germans, so it was decided we'd try for the airfield at Fornebu and get a plane. The roads were still clear and we had so far seen no traffic whatsoever. It was already daylight but the sky was still overcast. The Commander sat in front next to Sven the driver, whilst I sat in the back with the Chaplain and Ted, who remained pretty silent throughout the journey and most of the conversation and speculation was left to the other two and myself. At one stage, Sven pointed out the neat and attractive house of the composer, Grieg, and my remark that Solvega would really have had something to lament about had she been with us, really tickled him.

As we approached the airport, we became aware of the growing hum of approaching aircraft. Sven stopped the car and we got out to have a look. In the far distant sky above the road we had just come along, we could see several small groups of aircraft spread out across the sky. 'They're Germans. Come on. Let's get going!' said Sven. We got in quickly and started off at full speed. There were no side turnings to the road so we had to keep straight on.

We reached the airfield which was to the left of us. By now, the hum had grown into a roar of indescribable intensity. Sven pulled the car onto a verge by the side of the road under the shelter of some trees overhanging a low wall of a churchyard. We jumped out of the car, spread out and took what cover we could among the gravestones. I dropped behind the first upright tombstone I could find, grabbing it with my hands, hugging it close – squirming my body in a desperate attempt to get as much cover as I could. No matter how much I contorted my body, I was only too conscious of the fact that it was to be either my head and shoulders exposed, or my behind, and I couldn't help thinking what an awful calamity it would be to be shot in the rear. The first stream of bullets began to phut and zip around us. You could hardly hear them because of the deafening roar of the overhead aircraft. The very ground was vibrating and heaving to the noise. I had a glimpse of the deserted airfield beyond. Near us there seemed to be two tarpaulin-covered anti-aircraft guns, silent and deserted. On the far-distant perimeter I could make out an anti-aircraft gun surrounded by eight or nine moving figures. One moment the muzzle was emitting a series of quick flashes, and the next minute it was enveloped in one huge flash with bodies, earth and metal flying in all directions. I remember shouting to my companions, but the noise was too great for them to hear – a solid black of roaring engine noise. I looked up. I'd never seen anything like it! One gigantic swathe of planes flying almost tip to tip and blackening the sky. On and on they roared in a never-ending stream. The scene was awe-inspiring and frightening. Suddenly I realised what war was going to mean. 'God help the country,' I thought. Still they came on. There must have been hundreds and hundreds of planes. The whole ground was shaking. I'm sure they must have struck terror into the hearts of all who saw them. They epitomised to the full, the power. and might of the German invaders.

As the last of this vast armada flew off into the distance, we got up and scrambled back to the car. Luckily none of us had been injured and the car had suffered no damage. Our sense of urgency was now mounting. After a brief consultation, Sven decided we should carry on and make for Elverum, which meant bearing north-east instead of north-west to the coast.

At the first opportunity we left the main road and climbed the higher mountain roads that were still bedecked with snow. Occasionally we stopped to watch Germans speeding along on motor-bikes on the roads below. The bikes had side-cars with mounted machine-guns, with one occupant and a driver with a pillion rider on the back. They came along in small interspersed batches of six to eight with small carrier cars full of troops accompanying them every now and then. Beyond this, everything was still peaceful. Sven seemed to know his way well. How long we drove for was hard to calculate. We'd sight a small town or village in the distance, stop, and Sven would get out and check the lie of the land, bringing back food and information. It appeared that the Germans had not reached so far in force as yet, so we pressed on.

During the journey I was relating some of my experiences in Finland and Esthonia to Williams who asked me if I'd heard about the escape of the Polish submarine, *Orzel*, whilst I was over there. I told him how I was on my way through Esthonia when the *Orzel*, which had escaped capture by the Germans during the invasion of Poland, had put into the neutral port of Tallinn and had been interned. Subsequently, when I was in Riga, the capital of the neighbouring state of Latvia, I'd heard a lurid account of how the crew had killed the soldiers guarding her and had escaped with the submarine into the Baltic. The German colony's newspaper at that time had been very bitter about it and had accused the Esthonians of deliberately allowing the submarine to get away. He informed me that the *Orzel* was now with the British fleet and had just recently sunk a German ship, the *Rio de Janeiro*, off the Norwegian coast. I got the impression that this had something to do with his being in Norway, but I did not ask him.

It must have been four hours since we left the airfield when we came upon the first signs of a Norwegian resistance to the invasion. A group of Norwegian soldiers manning four machine-guns, straddled the road in front of us and we were commanded to stop and get out. Sven took over at once, explaining who we were and the usual show of passports helped matters. We gave them all the information we could, but before going on, Williams got Sven to explain to them that the position of their machine-guns would be useless against a frontal attack and that they had far better conceal them among the cover of the rocks above, to give a better command of the roadway. They saw the wisdom of this and began to deploy their defences on the slopes above the road. We rode on, and came to one of the villages before Elverum. Here we were made very welcome by the inhabitants who gave us food – I had my first taste of a sandwich made with minced raw meat. They too were eager for information, and in turn warned us that Lillehammer had already been taken by the Germans, who were fanning out southwards across our proposed path. It seemed we would never make it to Narvik.

To me it was now a case of getting out of Norway at all costs, so I asked Sven if he could take us to Sweden, hoping that the Germans would not invade there too. Sven reckoned he could, though it would involve the risks of going back to reach a point on the border which he knew. He said it was Medskogen on the Swedish side of the frontier. Everyone agreed, though we hadn't a clue where it was. So off we went. We could not have picked a finer saviour than Sven; he handled the car magnificently over those mountains and deeply wooded forests. We had arrived just outside the approach to the Swedish border when a car suddenly shot into view behind us, switching its lights on and off, and hooting at us – presumably to stop. Sven stepped on the accelerator and we slightly increased the distance between us. We were expecting to be shot at any moment and crouched down in our seats. We arrived at a long clearing in the forest, at the end of which was a striped red and white barrier manned by Swedish troops. They let us through and commanded us to stop and get out. We were immediately surrounded by soldiers and led to the Commandant's office. Looking back, I saw the car that had been following us had stopped at the barrier. There were German armed soldiers in it, but the Swedes would not let them through. The Commandant listened to our story and took our passports away. I asked him to contact the British Embassy in Stockholm for verification as to our identities. Sven, being Norwegian, was taken away, but not before all had thanked him. I, as an afterthought, asked for a piece of paper and wrote a letter addressed to 'Those British Authorities Concerned', explaining that my companions and self had been aided in our escape from Norway by Sven, who was a Norwegian officer and wished to serve with the British forces in defence of his country. This I signed as Security Officer to the British Legation in Norway, and gave it to Sven. Unfortunately, I never heard what happened to him.

After being held an hour or so, pending enquiries as to our identity, we were informed that everything was all right. We were then escorted to a small hotel, given rooms for the night and told we'd be put on a train for Stockholm the next morning.

Following a good night's rest, we reported back to the Commandant, our passports were returned and we were driven to the station. There was an obvious air of tension in Medskogen and there seemed to be an unusual number of uniformed police about for such a small town.

We were soon on our way to Stockholm, the journey lasting about four and a half hours. On arrival, we got a taxi and went straight to the Legation. The first person I met was Mr Lascelles. I was surprised to see him, being under the impression that by this time he would have been well on his way to England.

He congratulated me on my safe arrival and took me to the Minister to give an account of what had happened. When I had finished, the Minister smiled and said, 'It looks to me, Murray, the war is following you around. I think we'd better get you out of Stockholm before you bring trouble here too!'

I had barely been a week in Stockholm when I received instructions to report to the Secretary of the Legation. He called me into his room and told me to sit down. He himself stood up with a typical gesture that always amused me. He'd stand, legs apart, one hand in his trousers pocket, the other holding a chain with a bunch of keys attached to it, whirling them round and round.

'There's a couple of diplomatic bags that have to go tomorrow — one is to Helsinki, the other to the Legation in Riga. Which one do you wish to take? It's up to you, Murray.'

Now my mother and father were still in Riga and I was terribly anxious to see how they were getting on; to all intents and purposes, it was logical therefore, that I should opt for the Riga run. But throughout my life I have invariably depended and acted upon intuition. It's a peculiar sense which I cannot define, and in some cases it has led me into some right messes, but then again something invariably happens to get me out of them.

'I'll take the Helsinki bag!' I said.

'All right, report tomorrow at eight, Murray, and don't be late. The boat leaves at nine.'

I turned up at the Legation the next morning in good time and was joined by the other courier. I was pleased to find that I had only one diplomatic bag to look after, whilst my fellow courier had eight bulky bags. The diplomatic bags, made of stout canvas, were sealed and studded with large brass eyelets for the purpose of ensuring that they would sink quickly should the occasion arise for throwing them overboard in the event of an impending attack. Our instructions were always simple and to the point: 'Guard them with your life and prevent them getting into the hands of the enemy!'

My colleague and I were driven in the Legation car down to the quayside and we boarded our respective ships. I could not help envying my opposite number. His ship was spanking new. A Swedish liner of about five thousand tons, sleek, dazzling white with shining brasswork. Mine was a Finnish boat, a small five hundred tonner more like an old weather-beaten converted tug.

Our boats sailed off side by side. After a couple of hours' sailing, we had cleared the islands that surround Stockholm and steamed into the open Baltic. As we reached the point where our paths diverged, the Swedish liner bearing south, and my boat heading north, the grey form of a German destroyer cut right across our bows, her heliographs blinking frantically. With many of the Finnish crew standing beside me, we watched the Swedish ship slow down.

'He's after them,' the Finnish officer standing next to me said. 'Here have a look,' and he handed me his binoculars. Peering through them I could discern my colleague on the blind side of the ship to the destroyer, hurriedly tumbling the diplomatic bags into the sea. I saw a small boat with German sailors leave the destroyer and head for the Swedish ship. I did not see the end – we steamed on fast. One thing I do know, my colleague never arrived in Riga!

The rest of the voyage was uneventful. After about eight hours we arrived in Helsinki where I was met by one of the Minister's staff and whisked off to the Legation. After delivering my bag and reporting to the Chargé d'Affaires, I was told to return the next day for further instructions.

I found things in Finland were back to normal, the war with Russia having ended in March, so I went off to Desmond's place to stay the night. He was glad to see me again and looked none the worse for his sojourn in Helsinki during the war, and we had lunch together and swapped yarns. I was very happy to hear that his wife and children had managed to reach England safely and were well. I took the opportunity of visiting Mrs Paloheimo and was shocked to learn that her husband, Arvi, had died from a heart attack during one of the air-raids on Finland. Her son, however, who had been in the Army, was alive and well. I asked her about her father, Jean Sibelius. She told me he was still going strong, although he was now getting old and more crotchety than ever. She asked me if I got the message during the early days of the Russian attack, to go down and stay with them at their country home. She had made all the arrangements to put me up and was really upset I had not replied. I told her I had been staying in the Legation and had been suddenly sent to Sweden, which was the reason I'd not got her message, which had been directed to my flat.

The next day I returned to the Legation, where I was informed that there was a diplomatic bag to be taken to Tallinn, the capital of Esthonia. A seat had been booked for me on a plane that was leaving at six the following morning, and in view of the urgency, I was to sleep in the Legation that night, so as to be ready first thing. There seemed to be a lot of activity that night. Most of the senior staff were working all night. However, I managed to get some sleep, and was up and ready well before six.

I collected my 'bag' and was leaving with one of the staff detailed to accompany me to the airport when one of the secretaries came running down the steps and called us back. It appeared an urgent despatch had just come in from London and the decoding would still take some time, and I was not to leave until further instructions. Whatever it was, it took a further three hours. Additional despatches were put into my bag, it was resealed and I was then told that I was to leave on the cross-gulf steamer at noon. The journey across the Gulf of Finland took the boat about three hours and when we arrived in Tallinn I looked in vain for the Legation official who should have been there to meet me. Not seeing anyone, I hailed a taxi and was driven to the Legation. There was some consternation at my arrival, and I was taken immediately to the Minister, Mr Gallienne.

'Thank goodness you're alive, Murray! How did you get here?'

I told him about my delay in Helsinki, still somewhat mystified what all the fuss was about.

He explained that the last message they had received from Helsinki was that I'd left on the six o'clock plane for Tallinn. They had sent one of their staff to meet me, but had been informed at the aerodrome that the plane had mysteriously blown up whilst flying over the Gulf of Finland. There had been no survivors. It was known that the plane would be carrying French and Japanese couriers as well as myself, and several foreign journalists. My name had been on the list and they had not, as yet, received any signal from Helsinki that I had been re-routed hence their surprise at seeing me.

When I recounted to him what I had seen on the voyage from Stockholm, he said he had already heard about it. My colleague had been captured aboard the Swedish ship and taken off as a prisoner of war. This was one of the reasons why he would have to send me to Riga with duplicate despatches that same night. Later that evening, I was on the train to Latvia looking forward to meeting my parents again, so much had happened since I had last seen them. On the morning of 10 June 1940, I arrived in Riga.

Part III

War comes to Latvia

The Soviet Secret Police
Move In

I was met at the station by one of the junior members of the diplomatic staff and driven to the Riga Legation. I handed over my diplomatic bag and after quickly finishing with the necessary formalities and receiving instructions to stand by until called for, I hurried off to surprise my parents.

It was quite a reunion. They were relieved and overjoyed at seeing me. Soon I was sitting down again to a home-cooked meal. They were, of course, anxious to know what had been happening to me. I gave them a sketchy account, making everything sound like a normal course of duty. I did not want them to get unduly worried. Latvia was still a peaceful country and as far as outward appearances were concerned, the actual war was still far beyond their borders, though by now I was already beginning to have my doubts as to how long this would remain so.

It was nice to see some of the old faces again and as my passport was completely filled with visa stamps, I called on Glynn Hall the Vice-Consul, to get it renewed. I had known him since 1925 when I'd first come to Riga. In the course of our meeting, I mentioned that since arriving back I had seen a letter addressed to one of my acquaintances from his brother who had left Latvia for Germany and on arriving there had been enrolled in the German Army. His brother had written that he was in Peenamund, a German coastal resort in the Baltic, and his unit were carrying out exercises on the sands in preparation for desert warfare.

He did not give this information much credence, however, because at the time it did not look as though Hitler had any thoughts, or reasons, whatsoever, to embark on desert warfare.

A few days later I was called to the Legation for an interview with the Chargé d'Affaires.

'We've received a request from the Embassy in Moscow to send them a secretary for duty with the Air Attaché, Murray. Would you like to go?'

Although taken by surprise at this unexpected offer, I replied without hesitation, 'Yes, I'll go.' My assent must have been expected because I was immediately presented with a series of prepared documents for me to sign. Amongst them was a short form stipulating that as my appointment was a war-time emergency one, I would not be entitled to compensation for disablement or even loss of life incurred during the term of my employment. In other words, I took the job on at my own risk.

On querying this document, I was told that owing to the recent Soviet–German pact, His Majesty's Government could no longer guarantee the safety of its personnel on Soviet territory. I signed. The Legation undertook to procure the necessary Soviet entry visa and Latvian exit permit on my completing the application forms and supplying four photographs. I had always taken the precaution of carrying several passport photographs about with me, so there was no delay in getting that part of the procedure under way. The Ambassador in Moscow, however, had to confirm my appointment, so I was told to call back in a couple of days for final instructions.

It was with mixed feelings that I went home to acquaint my parents with the news. They took it well and we spent most of that evening speculating what it would be like to live in Moscow.

During the morning of 14 June 1940, we had an unexpected visitor – it was Mrs Rhodes, one of my mother's old friends who was married to a Latvian. She was full of excitement and as I let her into the flat she cried, 'Have you heard the news? The Bolsheviks are here. They've invaded Latvia! Oh dear, whatever will happen to us now?' and she began to weep.

I looked at my mother and father. I did not know what to say. I just felt as though the pit of my stomach was dropping out. Suddenly my mother put her arms around her old friend, 'There dear, don't go on so, it'll be all right! I'll make a cup of tea. Sit down now, there's no need to go on so.'

Finally we quietened Mrs Rhodes down. I assured her there

would be no fighting and said I would go along with my father to watch the Russians march in, as it was bound to be a peaceful occupation and the Russians were not as bad as everyone thought they were.

Deep down inside me, though, my mind was in a whirl – the news was a shock. First Finland, then Norway, then the unbelievable news about France and Dunkirk! England itself threatened and now here, a thousand miles away from home. How was it all going to end?

I asked Mrs Rhodes how she had come to hear that the Russians were coming, and was it really true because everything outside appeared to be quiet and normal. She said she'd been round to see Mrs Bisseniek, an Englishwoman who was also married to a Latvian, who had told her that her husband had been called away in the night and had not returned home. Someone had telephoned her that very morning from the Finance Ministry to say her husband was being kept at the Ministry as the Russians were expected to march into Riga during the afternoon. She had left Mrs Bisseniek in a state of collapse and had come round to tell us the news.

I could well imagine the state Mrs Bisseniek would be in as she had good cause to fear for his safety. George Bisseniek had been the Latvian Consul in Leningrad when one of Stalin's right-hand men, Sergei Mironovitch Kirov, had been assassinated. The date was 1 December 1934. The man who shot Kirov was a Leonid Nikolayev who was said to have received aid from a foreign Consul on behalf of a 'Great Power' in order to carry out the deed. The official Soviet newspaper *Izvestia* quoted Bisseniek as being the mysterious Consul behind the affair. Bisseniek, whom I knew personally, later told me there was no truth in the allegation. What had happened was that following the assassination he had received an anonymous telephone call from a supposed well-wisher informing him that he was going to be arrested by the GPU* (The Soviet Secret Police) and charged with complicity in Kirov's

* Readers should note that the Soviet State Security Department came under headings denoted by the following initials:

From 1922–34	– GPU
From 1934–43	– NKVD
From 1943–46	– NKGB
From 1946–53	– MGB
From 1953–onwards	– KGB

murder. He was told it would be advisable to get out of Leningrad as quickly as possible. Fearing for his life he left by train that very night and returned to Latvia. The next day *Izvestia* published an article claiming that the guilty man was the Latvian Consul who had already fled the country to avoid interrogation and Soviet justice.

Mrs Bisseniek's fears proved to be well-founded, her husband was never to return home again. He was the first of many people I knew in Riga that were later to disappear.

Mrs Rhodes stayed for lunch and feeling a good deal better, went off to see Mrs Bisseniek again, while my father and I went off to watch the arrival of the Russian troops.

Everything was quiet in the streets; the shops were open. The only thing that was noticeable was that there were no trams running along the *Marijas Iela* so we had to walk to the centre of the town. There were also no uniformed soldiers to be seen. This was unusual because Latvia had a large conscript Army and there were always quite a number of soldiers to be seen on the streets.

As we reached the end of the *Marijas Iela*, near the railway station, we were halted by a huge crowd of some twenty thousand or more people lining both sides of the street and spilling over on to the green verge to the left of the National Theatre. We were soon parted by the jostling, thrusting crowd, and I found myself being pushed along with the mass of people near the theatre. We had arrived just on time. Cheers and hurrahs filled the air as the first tanks came rumbling by. Over the heads of the crowd I could see the open turrets of the tanks as they swept by in one unending roar. The soldiers standing in the turrets were of small build and had swarthy Mongolian features. They looked neither right or left, staring with impassive faces straight ahead, completely ignoring the waving and cheering of the Latvians. The crowd was constantly surging backwards and forwards, breaking the thin cordon of police strung along the sides of the street. This went on for some time, when without warning, a sudden volley of shots were fired over the heads of the crowd. Those I was with panicked. Gratings surrounding the National Theatre were torn up, and before I knew where I was, I found myself jammed in one of the large manholes. With another volley of bullets spluttering overhead I could not see what was happening, but could still hear the tanks roaring on and the crowd cheering, booing and cat-calling intermittently. The firing stopped and the crowd once again surged forward to greet the tanks, whilst I jumped out of the manhole and searched the outskirts of the crowd for my father. Deciding that he had already gone home, I gave up the search and started off at the double, anxious to get back as soon as I could. To avoid the crowds, I made my way through Verman's Park adjoining the Boulevard. I passed groups of machine-guns manned by tense-faced Homeguards (The *Aizsargi*) lying in the grass, their guns trained on the approaches to the park. What they were doing there I did not know; and from the looks of them, they did not know either. Leaving the park I came into the streets which were this time quite deserted. I began to run and did not stop running until I reached home. I was relieved to find Dad had arrived before me. Sensibly, he had made his way back shortly after we had been parted. We stayed up very late that night, but all was quiet, the people in the surrounding flats and houses remaining indoors.

The next morning Dad went off to work early and I went to the Legation. Life seemed normal and the shops were open as usual.

I found the Legation staff busily emptying filing cabinets and burning documents – it was the Norwegian Legation all over again. From a short conversation I had with the Secretary, I gathered all Legations and Consulates throughout Latvia had been given forty-eight hours to get out by the Russians who were in the process of annexing the Baltic States for their 'protection' as the Secretary grimly put it. When I asked what was going to happen to the rest of the British colony in Latvia, he said Glynn Hall the Vice-Consul would be left in charge, he being the only British official that the Russians would allow to remain until arrangements for evacuation had been completed by our Embassy in Moscow. He also informed me that our Embassy had confirmed my appointment, my visas had been applied for and I would be notified by the Soviet Embassy and the Riga Police Prefectura when they would be ready. All I had to do was to sit tight until I received their notification.

From the Legation I went to the British Club where I thought I might see someone with whom I could discuss the situation. The only one there was John Watson, a British timber merchant. He was a very knowledgeable chap and always seemed one ahead with all the news. He'd heard that the Colony would be evacuated to Vladivostock and thence to Australia. He said he was not surprised the Russians had been welcomed as most of the crowd would be the industrial workers who belonged to the communist-inspired Stradnieku party. He showed me the *Jaunakas Zinios* (the Latvian national newspaper). It gave a lurid account of the previous day's shooting. 'A brutal attack by the Fascist-inspired police against innocent workers who had assembled to greet their Soviet brothers and saviours,' was how they put it. It went on to say that fifteen unarmed workers had been killed before the 'authorities' could take action. 'Justice would be demanded by the workers and they could rest assured that all necessary steps would be taken to bring the guilty fascist police to book for their dastardly actions.' Other articles stressed the united efforts of all peace-loving workers and their leaders to bring the war-mongering fascist element of the former government to justice.

When I left Watson I promised to return that evening for a dinner in honour of some of the Legation staff who were leaving. It was at this dinner that I met Mr Reinhardt, a young American cipher officer passing through Riga on his way to join the American Embassy in Moscow. He had already received his visas and was due to travel with those of our Embassy staff leaving for Moscow. We had quite a friendly chat and I promised to look him up when I arrived there. The next day I went to see them all off, but was not allowed to approach the platform. The railway station was already under close guard and long queues of people with their bags and bundles were waiting about for trains to take them to their various destinations. But only those with special permits were being allowed to leave Riga.

The days passed by. I still awaited news concerning my visas. During this time changes became evident all round. My father told me that the directors in the factory had all disappeared. No one knew what had happened to them. A Commissar had been appointed to the factory whose job it was to organise 'Work Committees' and convene workers' meetings. Measures were taken to ensure that the factory worked at full blast. It was compulsory for every worker to attend these meetings at which Marxist principles were expounded and the role of the Soviets in freeing the proletariat were acclaimed. Even my father who could not understand the language had to be in attendance. Marches and parades were also organised with the workers from other factories to take place on the official rest days. They were held to show the populace the solidarity and happiness of the working class. I occasionally took my mother to watch these processions and we'd cheer my father as he trudged along, hanging on to a ribbon streamer attached to one of the many huge banners depicting Lenin and Stalin. In the evenings we would pull his leg about it. But it was a thing he dared not avoid. Workers in the factory who had stubbornly refused to take part in spite of being cautioned, disappeared and were not seen again.

To all intents and purposes the banks were closed and assets frozen. Only the paying of money and limited withdrawals were allowed, while paper money became more evident.

The markets my mother used were no longer filled with innumerable stalls and tables packed with mounds of vegetables, meat, butter and other dairy produce. Instead, they gradually diminished in number and there were now only miserable small portions of everything to be seen.

On the first day the jewellers shops, of which there had been many in Riga, were locked and guarded by roughly-clad civilians wearing red armbands and armed with bayonetted rifles. The shop windows were later emptied of all jewellry and one saw them replaced with one or two shoddy alarm clocks. The big stores, one especially, the *Armijas Ekonomiskas Veikals*, were besieged by Russian soldiers purchasing everything which they could lay their hands on. They seemed to have enormous sums of Latvian paper money in their possession. The stores were soon empty. In the streets quite a large number of Russians appeared, dressed in drab khaki tunics over which they wore a Sam Brown belt and holstered revolver, with baggy trousers tucked into leather knee-length field boots. They looked and seemed to act quite kindly towards the civilian population.

I often saw them sitting on benches in the Boulevard and Parks, quietly discussing and explaining the political situation to groups of ordinary citizens who would gather around them listening intently. These were the 'politicos' whose job it was to smooth over the Occupation. On the surface, life seemed to be proceeding in a well-ordered fashion. Perhaps it was because the working element of the population was kept intensely busy, all factories and industries having been ordered to carry on as usual, with the emphasis on higher production.

During the second week of the Russian Occupation, I received a telegram from Moscow. It simply read, 'Please report without delay for duty at the British Embassy Moscow – (signed) Stafford Cripps.' I decided to take the telegram and go immediately to the Prefectura and Soviet Embassy to enquire about my visas. The Police Prefectura was a large stone building just off the Boulevard and was the centre of Police administration for the whole of Riga and its suburbs. The place was packed, every ante-room was filled with men and women waiting for permits of one sort or another. Some seeking news of relatives who had disappeared; some endeavouring to procure travelling permits, and others identity documents. Armed soldiers guarded all doors and kept the crowds in order. The fact that I was a British diplomatic official counted for nothing. On managing, after much difficulty, to reach one of the inner offices, the telegram was taken from me and I was told to wait. I was put into a small waiting room by myself. After half an hour, a man in officer's uniform came in and said brusquely in English, 'Your papers are being attended to, but you must go to the Soviet Embassy, who will deal with your Soviet visa.' He gave me no chance to discuss the matter but summoned a soldier to escort me out of the building.

The Soviet Embassy was a huge white building set in its own grounds in another boulevard, running at right angles to the main boulevard, which contained many fine, imposing edifices, the former homes of the wealthy. They looked, with their shuttered windows, totally deserted. My reception at the Embassy was similar to that at the Prefectura. An impassive official took my telegram, asked if I spoke Russian to which I said no, and then questioned me in German, which I understood. His answer was brief. 'Your application is being dealt with, call again next week.'

I left and went to the main Post Office and sent a telegram to the

Embassy in Moscow stating why I was held up. This was only one of the many telegrams I was subsequently permitted to send to Moscow. Only later was I to find out that the Embassy never received them.

Three days after this, at six o'clock on the evening of 9 July, I was sitting in the flat with my parents having tea when there came a knock at the door. I opened it. Two men stood outside.

They were an unusal looking couple. One was an elderly man of small compact build, grey-haired, clean-shaven, wearing metal-rimmed spectacles behind which a pair of slate grey eyes fixed me with an unblinking stare. His face was long and narrow, the skin ashy-grey, but heavily pitted with pock marks. The other man was younger, about thirty-five years of age, heavily built, with a large full-moon face, also clean-shaven. He had the swarthy look of a Georgian Russian with large round black eyes, longish straight hair which was black and greasy. He wore an ordinary working man's check cloth cap on his head. Both, however, wore grey gaberdine coats, much too long for them, and their shoes were long and very pointed in the fashion of the 'twenties'. They seemed to glide rather than walk normally.

It was the younger man who addressed me, 'Are you Mister Murray?' He spoke English with a heavy American, nasal twang.

'Yes,' I nodded.

'Can we talk with you?' he said.

'Yes, come in,' I invited. I took them in and introduced them to my parents. My mother instantly offered them a cup of tea, but they refused. They sat down with their headgear still on. I asked what I could do for them. It was the younger man who continued:

'Can you speak Russian?' he enquired.

Although I knew a fair amount of Russian, I decided on the spur of the moment to say no, but added, I could speak German besides English. I also complimented him on his perfect English, which I noted pleased him. 'My companion does not speak English, only Russian,' he said, and the other man evidently understanding, nodded his head in agreement. He went on. 'We are from the Russian tobacco industry and heard you have a tobacco factory in this country.'

'I did have, but not now,' I answered.

'But you know about Russian tobaccos, don't you?'

'Oh, yes, I used them in my tobacco blends. The Yalta, Souchoum, Namhun and Kuban are the best Russian tobaccos I know of and they make very good cigarettes,' I replied, wanting to appear friendly. He translated my remarks to his companion and they both smiled approvingly. The younger man then looked at his watch and said,

'We have to go now, but we would like to talk further with you. Perhaps we could have dinner together tonight – Yes?'

Not wishing to appear rude to my unexpected guests, I thanked them for their invitation and although feeling somewhat uneasy, was nevertheless curious to find out what they meant by 'further talk'. We shook hands and as they left, the spokesman for the two turned to me and said, 'Good, we will call for you tonight at eleven o'clock and we shall have a nice evening together.'

After they had gone, my father remarked, 'They're a couple of queer customers, aren't they?'

'Yes,' I said, 'they are queer customers, but they're Russians and things being what they are, it's as well to keep on the right side of them, anyway.'

I explained to my parents that they were Russian tobacco industrialists and that they had invited me out to dinner that night. When I said they were calling for me at eleven, they remarked that it was a pretty odd hour of night for dinner. They would have thought it odder still had they known what I knew! My unease had been caused by the fact that in listing the names of the Russian tobaccos I had mentioned the name 'Namhun' which was a Chinese tobacco leaf and one which any tobacco man would have known was not Russian. They had not even commented on this fact. So, they were not tobacco industrialists.

At eleven o'clock sharp, there was a knock at our door and there were my two guests to take me out. Waiting outside the house was a large black limousine complete with chauffeur. 'This is our car, we'll ride to the restaurant, nice and comfortable, eh!' my companion said. We drove through the by now quiet and deserted streets to the centre of the city and stopped outside the Caucasia restaurant. This was a basement restaurant well known for its cuisine. You went down steps, along a passage leading to a large circular room, surrounded by a series of intimate alcoves across which curtains could be drawn. The centre of the dance floor had a raised platform for the orchestra. The furnishings were rich and lush, the lighting soft. It was a notorious locale for tired businessmen and their lady friends. This night, however, although the orchestra of five performers was playing, the place seemed deserted. We were conducted to an alcove by a very attentive waiter and sat down to a table already loaded with a choice selection of hors d'oeuvres. The remainder of the meal consisted of steaks of fresh salmon with all the trimmings, followed by ice-cream and coffee. The only time my hosts smiled was when I insisted on only drinking tonic water instead of the spirits and wines that were offered.

They really enjoyed their food and were not sparing with the drink either. I enjoyed mine, too, in spite of feeling a bit queasy. In the beginning, the conversation was just a series of commonplace remarks which, in between gaps, had to be translated and relayed back and forth. Nothing was mentioned about tobaccos and I was beginning to wonder what this meeting was all about when suddenly I was asked if I would like to work for the Soviet tobacco industry? To this unexpected question, I replied that much as I might like to, I was already engaged by my government to work at the British Embassy in Moscow and was awaiting daily my visas. There was a long pause and the younger man fixed me with a steady stare. 'We know all about you!' This abrupt change in manner and tone had me non-plussed.

'What has that to do with me,' I countered. 'I don't know anything about you, not even your names.'

He ignored my interruption and repeated, 'Yes, we know all about you. You were in Koenigsberg in July 1930; in December the same year you were in Berlin——' and without pausing, went on to rattle off dates and names of various cities and countries I had visited during the past ten years, many of which I had already forgotten about. The details were amazing. I was quite taken aback at this sudden change in the conversation and was beginning to wonder where it was all leading to. I interrupted him and said, 'Look here, I don't know what you're talking about. Anywhere I have been is my business. What has it got to do with you?'

'No? But I only want to show you that we know all about you. Everything!'

With that he banged the table service bell. A waiter appeared, the older man scribbled on a chit of paper, gave it to him and was dismissed by a wave of his hand. They then both rose from the table, simply said, 'Goodnight,' and left me sitting there. Just like that, one word and they were gone. I wondered what was going to happen next. I looked at my watch; it was already three a.m. I got up and walked out. As I made my way home through the deserted streets, I heard the sound of footsteps coming from some distance behind me. I surmised I was being followed, but try as I would, I could not get a glimpse of my follower. Our house was in a kind of cul-de-sac off the *Artillerijas Iela*. An armed soldier stood on duty at the top of the street. He made no move to stop me as I passed and just gave me a cursory glance. I had a feeling of disquiet, nevertheless, as it dawned upon me that now our street was under surveillance.

Over a week went by and still I could get no news about the granting of my visas and visits to the Soviet Embassy were met with curt dismissals. Once I observed the figure of the elder man framed in a top window of the Embassy watching me when I called. I became aware also that I was being followed whenever I went out. The armed soldier was still evident at the top of the street; even my mother noticed him. I told mother not to worry as it was for our protection. It was an assurance I did not feel. Our house which contained fifteen flats was now almost empty – the occupants had, one by one, been collected on various nights. The procedure had always been the same. At about midnight, a covered lorry would come noisily down the street, six or seven armed soldiers would jump out and enter the house. We would hear banging and shouting through the curtains, and we'd see our former neighbours helped into the lorry – a few bundles thrown in after them and off the lorry would go again. We never knew much about them beyond the fact that they were some kind of civil servants, mostly youngish couples, who kept very much to themselves. The atmosphere was unpleasant and though we did not talk about it, I knew my parents were feeling the strain, and this was one of the reasons why I did not go out much. I was frightened something might happen whilst I was out. The landlord who had always collected the rent personally, also disappeared and in his place a house porter was appointed to collect the rent and live in one of the flats. This man appeared one day with a house book which we had to sign stating name, nationality, place of birth, and place of employment.

I received another telegram from Moscow. It was from the Embassy stating that I should report for immediate duty urgently. No mention was made of my previous explanatory telegram to them. I went to the Post Office and tried to telephone the Embassy, but they said there was no telephone communication with Moscow, but I could send a telegram, which I did, guardedly explaining that I was still awaiting my exit visa from Latvia and the Soviet Embassy's entry visa for Moscow; adding that they should try and hurry things up for me over there. As the days went by, I began to feel despondent. Somehow I knew that my telegrams were not reaching Moscow, but why were the telegrams from Moscow being permitted to reach me? It was a question I could not answer. Every time I went to the Prefectura and the Soviet Embassy I was either deliberately fobbed off with some excuse and passed on from one official to another or requested to call at a later date. It was an impasse I could not break through. Sometimes I was not even allowed to enter the buildings which teemed with armed military-clad officials.

I called occasionally at the British Club which was also depressing. There were reports that the Club was to be shut down, but the Secretary declared he would remain in residence and never leave, stoutly maintaining it was British property, built on British soil. This was quite true, the English Church and adjoining Club had been built with materials and on soil brought specially over from England many years ago by members of the British Colony to ensure that there would always be a little part of England on the shores of the Baltic.

No one there had any news from the Embassy in Moscow: all communications for the time being dead.

I was returning from the Club one afternoon when I met my two Russians at the top of our street. I greeted them and they stopped me. The young man shook my hand and said, 'We are going to call for you tonight and we shall have a nice dinner, you understand?' The last bit was said in quite an authoritative tone.

I just nodded. I felt more depressed than ever. These were not ordinary people. It was very disturbing and all I could do was wait and see what it was all about.

Again they called for me at eleven o'clock at night. The car was the same and we drove to the same restaurant as before. There was no orchestra playing at the Caucasia that evening. All was silent and deserted. We spoke very little during the meal which consisted of several courses of the most extravagant food, superbly cooked and served. The two Russians were good trenchermen and obviously enjoyed their food. I still refused wine and spirits and stuck to soft drinks which again made them smile. No reference was made to our previous dinner, and I was racking my brain to think up something to keep the conversation going when the elder man, who as usual had hardly spoken a word, turned to his companion and said in Russian, 'Enough, give it to him hard, we have wasted enough time already!' I gave no indication that I had understood what had been said, and waited enquiringly for the younger man to translate what had been said, knowing full well he would not. He sat back, took out a packet of cigarettes, offered me one which I accepted, took one himself, and we lit up. Then, turning to me, said, 'We know everything about you.'

'Well, what of it, you've told me that before.'

Ignoring my remark, he continued, 'You are poor, we can give you much money.' He waved his cigarette expansively, 'Anywhere in the world, London, New York, South America, in any currency you like.' He waited to see what I would say. There was nothing for me to say other than the obvious.

'You say you are going to give me money, eh, and what have I to do for this money?'

He spoke very slowly, 'You are going to your Embassy in Moscow, yes? You will be doing much writing in your work; it is nothing, just simple – you make an extra copy of your work and we shall collect it and pay you much money, anywhere, to any bank you like.'

I felt sick. Then this was what it was all about. I was in the hands of the Russian secret service. I felt cornered, isolated. The proposition was monstrous. I decided to put up a show and brazen it out. I stood up, and fear gave way to an uncontrollable fit of anger.

'See here, I don't want to know what you are talking about. Also, I don't want to know you, and I wish I'd never met you,' I shouted, and with that strode to the curtains and tore them apart to get out. Two soldiers with crossed rifles and bayonets barred my path. The younger man leapt to his feet, towering above me he put one hand on my shoulder and flung me back into my seat, whilst the other calmly got up and drew the curtains to again.

'We are talking to you – you understand? This is not the time for comic operatics. Listen to what I have to say——' I interrupted him,

'Yes, you want me to be a traitor to my country.'

'Your country, pah! you are not even British,' he countered.

'Yes, I am. I was born and bred in England and it is my country.'

'Ah, born and bred in England,' he mimicked. 'If you're born in a stable that doesn't make you a donkey.'

'Well, look at you, you're not even proper Russians,' I countered. He ignored this gibe and spread out his hands placatingly.

'Don't be silly, this is business, a simple business proposition, what is the reason for getting angry about it? Just be calm and think about it. Perhaps you will change your mind. What have you to lose? Your country, Great Britain is finished. The Germans have beaten your armies and soon they will invade your country.'

'No,' I said. 'There are tens of millions of people in Britain, much better than me and they will not only fight, but in the end they will defeat Germany.'

'It is not so, your country is finished. It is us, the Soviets who will smash Germany, and it is so. Only the armies of the Soviet will defeat the German barbarians, and then you English will be our friends! Think again. What have you to lose?'

'I have nothing more to say,' I said, and shook my head and relapsed into a sullen silence.

The two men carried on a rapid discussion in a dialect I could not understand. Finally, the older man took out a piece of paper from his pocket, gave it to his companion who handed it to me with a fountain pen.

'We will not waste any more time with you,' he said. 'You will write down on this paper what I dictate to you and sign it with your name.'

'I am not writing or signing anything,' I said.

'You will do as I say or you do not leave here. Do you understand that?'

I knew that there was no way out of the situation. Besides, I felt tired and sick with worry.

'All right, tell me what you want me to write.'

He dictated slowly and I wrote the following:

'I, John Murray, the undersigned, will not communicate or divulge to anyone the meetings and conversations I have had with the representatives of the Soviet Union Tobacco Industry. Should I do so, then I understand that I will be liable for whatever punishment will be carried out against me.' I paused before signing it.

'Go on, sign your name.'

'No,' I said, 'I will sign it if it is necessary, but first you must promise me that I will get my visas without any more trouble, so that I can join my Embassy in Moscow. As you have said this is a private business matter between us, I won't mention it to anyone – not even to my superiors, and I always keep my word.'

'Don't worry, you'll get your visas, but you must sign the paper now. We are not waiting here all night.'

I signed.

The pock-faced man took the paper, folded it up and put it in his pocket wallet. We rose from the table, the younger man escorted me past the sentries who stood rigidly to attention, and at the door he stopped and put his hand on my shoulder.

'Don't worry, everything will be all right, but think carefully. You love your mother and father; it would not be pleasant for them to be sent to a labour camp. Think about it, and let us know when you meet us again. We shall wait for you in the restaurant at Verman's Park at eight o'clock on Sunday evening. Do not be late!' With that he ushered me out.

My head swam as I walked the deserted streets. It was four a.m. and already beginning to get light. I neither cared nor feared whether I was followed that morning. The whole situation was so unreal, except the threat uttered about Mum and Dad. That was real. I thought about the paper I'd signed – I had really meant it when I said I would tell no one, but would they keep their promise about getting my visas granted?

Once in Moscow I'd have the Embassy to help me, but would they now let me go? Deep down inside I knew the Russians would not keep their promise; the only consolation I had was that it would at least free me from mine. But what could I do? I hadn't the faintest idea.

The days that followed were a nightmare. I jumped at every knock at the door and shivered when a car came down the street. I accompanied my mother every time she went out shopping and waited anxiously every day for my father's return from work. Meanwhile, I had to hide my anxiety from them. They, poor souls, never lacked courage but I did not want to add further to their unspoken fears about the future. Nevertheless, we managed to hold on to our bit of sense of humour, chivvying Dad about his procession, and Mam singing, 'He bore on high a banner bearing a strange device Excelsior, Excelsior!' Sometimes I'd say – 'I don't know what we are doing stuck in this place,' and my mother would remark, 'It's a funny old world John, but don't worry, it'll all come out right in the end.'

We had a Telefunken radio and the news was not always bright, but Churchill's speeches and the link with England gave us great comfort. All radios, by the way, were supposed to have been handed in to the authorities. I said that as we were foreigners and couldn't understand the various decrees that were made, we'd just plead ignorance if anyone came about our set. We were never troubled on this score, however.

It was by now the end of August – the five days to my next meeting with the Russians soon passed.

As I was getting ready to go out that evening, my mother asked me where I was going, and I told her that I had to meet our 'queer friends' at Verman's Park Restaurant. As I was going out, my mother looked at me searchingly, 'Well, John, be careful now, and don't do anything you would be ashamed of afterwards!'

I arrived at the Verman's Park Restaurant dead on time. This was a popular restaurant set in the midst of a small park adjacent to the State Opera House. Though many of the cafés and restaurants were closed, this one was still open. Not surprisingly, there were very few people in it, and I sat down at a corner table and ordered a lemonade. It was not that I was a teetotaller, it was just that a clear head seemed to me the most important thing. I waited. The minutes passed by. It was already half-past eight. I kept a watch on the doors and looked round at the other tables and still my Russians did not appear. I was wondering about this when a very young and most attractive young woman, heavily perfumed, with a glass of wine in her hand, glided up to my table.

'Can I sit at your table?' she asked, in faultless German. 'You look so miserable sitting there alone. Perhaps you would like to dance?' It was so obvious. I guessed at once that she had appeared in place of my two Russians, so I decided to play up to her for the time being.

The dances in those days were the tangos and foxtrots. You held your partner in your arms – close or otherwise as occasion demanded. This was a foxtrot – she held me close, with soft perfumed hair brushing my cheek. Her body was soft. Our steps seemed to match perfectly. Her dress, low cut but long, was of a blue silky material that clung close to the shape of her figure. We returned to our seats and after I had offered her a cigarette, she looked appealingly at me from out of a pair of soft limpid brown eyes, 'I'm so tired, would you like to see me home, we could perhaps have a little drink together?'

So my suspicions were confirmed. I thought it best to get out as quickly as possible. I looked at my watch. 'I'm sorry, thank you for your kind invitation, but I have to meet someone and am late already.' With that, without waiting for any comment, I got up quickly and went home.

The following day another telegram arrived from the Embassy in Moscow: 'Cannot understand your delay in reporting for duty stop you are to proceed to Moscow immediately – Stafford Cripps.' I decided to send an answer, once again explaining my difficulties with my travel permits, and then proceed to the Prefectura to complain about the delay in granting my visas. Arriving at the Prefectura I demanded to see the head of the Visa Department. This time I was told to remain in the waiting room, which was packed with Latvian subjects, mostly poorly clad, some holding small babies and others bundles which I supposed contained all their earthly belongings. From what I heard in the hubbub of conversation going on, many had been waiting weeks for permission to return to their homes in the country. I had to wait nearly two hours before a policeman came to escort me to a room deep in the interior of the building.

We had to pass through endless guarded corridors to reach the room. Before me sat a high-ranking officer at a table on which were a file and a pile of papers. There was also a large black revolver lying on the table to the left of him. He spoke in English.

'What do you want?' he snapped. I told him I was from the British Diplomatic Service and had come about my visa to Moscow.

'You get no visa from here. You are a spy!' he shouted.

'Me, a spy? Don't be ridiculous. You know it's not true!'

'Yes, you are a spy – a German spy, and you will be shot!'

I was shaken. 'If you touch me, you will be held responsible by my Embassy –' I began. But he interrupted me, shouting –

'Yes, you are spying for the Germans. We have the papers to prove you are a double agent and when we have shot you, we will send the documents to your Embassy to prove it. They will be only too pleased to know we have found you out. Do you understand what I say?'

It was my death sentence, I knew it! My knees seemed to be buckling from under me. But the one dominant thought that overrode all others was that at all costs I must not betray the fear I felt.

'Go on, shoot me then. Shoot me now,' I blurted out in desperation.

'No, we'll shoot you when we are ready, not when you want,' he sneered.

'You go home now,' he commanded.

With that I was led out of the building without another word being spoken.

When I got home I went straight to my room and locked the door. I wanted to be alone. I tried to recall all the events leading to the situation I was in. The fact that I could be hauled off at any time, shot in the back of the head and dumped in some God-forsaken hole was terrifying enough, but what of my parents? Poor, innocent, harmless old folk, no one to help them. What *would* happen to them? I felt on the verge of insanity. I could see no way of escape – only the black horror of it all.

Now I am not religious in the accepted sense. I believe in God. A church of any denomination is to me the same – a place where one goes to commune with oneself in silence. My philosophy from being quite a young man had been that we and everything are one with God; we are part of God and of Him, and we should live according to the light of the conscience we have been given. For those that require ritual, let them be; for those that require hymns and music, let them be; for all is the creation of God's expression. In my case, I had devised a technique, which I used whenever I had reached the uttermost depths of hopeless despair. I had first used it in 1932 to blot out my grief when on returning home I found my sister laid out dead, the first close death that I had ever experienced. It was such a shock, so unexpected, she was gone, never to be recalled. I had recourse to use it again on a winter flight to Finland in 1938 when as a lone passenger in a small de Havilland biplane flying over the gulf of Finland in a blinding snowstorm, buffeted by the winds, we ran into trouble and chances of survival were minimal. The technique I used was to sing silently to myself over and over again my own version of the first two lines of the hymn –

> Oh God our help in ages past our hope
> for years to come. . . .
> For never ending Thou art God and our
> eternal hope.   Amen.

I sang this continually until my mind was conditioned to a state of mute nothingness, and so I would go on and on until nothing seemed to matter any more. When I returned once again to normality I always found that I could carry on in a kind of ice-cold logical manner that would brook no deviation either to the right or left of the path I decided to take. This may seem in a way callous, but it was the only way I knew of effecting a complete shutting out of all thoughts that could disturb my mental balance. It was a technique I only used in times of extreme urgency. I now called on it again to relieve the pressure I was feeling. 'Don't think about anything, John,' I said to myself. 'Nothing can touch you . . . Oh God our help . . .'

Two hours later I felt as if I was another person. I felt a kind of superiority to everyone and everything around me. So, the Russians had broken their promise to me! Now it was my turn. I felt a kind of righteous freedom to act in the way I thought correct. Up to this moment I had been afraid to meet or speak with anyone in case it would precipitate further action by the Soviet Agents and bring trouble to anyone I spoke to. It was for this reason I had avoided contact with any of my friends since the two mysterious Russians had called upon me. I decided I'd go and see Glynn Hall and tell him the whole story. I arrived at the Legation building without hindrance. It seemed deserted, so I banged hard on the door. It was opened by Mrs Glynn Hall herself. She looked very distraught and her eyes were puffed with recent tears.

'Oh, Mr Murray, I'm so glad to see you. Come in,' she cried.

'Can I see Glynn? It's very important,' I said.

'But he's ill, very ill. Oh I'm glad you've come. I don't know what to do with him.' And she burst into tears.

I followed her into one of the rooms. It was bare with just one long table in the centre. In the far corner of the room, crouched and doubled up, swaying from side to side, his hands clasped around his head, was Glynn Hall. He was whimpering, 'Don't let them get me! Don't let them take me away!' On and on he repeated the same words. I went over to him and patted his shoulder. 'Don't worry old chap, it's only me, Murray – no one will get you.' His eyelids were moving up and down in one continuous flicker – he could not look at me as he kept repeating the same thing until his voice dropped to an unintelligible mumble. He did not even recognise me. It was unbelievable! I saw that it would be hopeless to try and get any normal response from him. I turned to Mrs Hall and asked her how he came to be in such a state. She told me that some weeks previously, two strange men had called upon them. They were closeted with her husband for some time. When they left, she had found him in a state of collapse. Since then he had attempted to commit suicide and she had to watch over him all the time. I asked her if anyone from our own people had called, and she mentioned John Watson who had been very helpful and was a constant visitor. As he was what I called a 'senior member' of the British colony in Riga, I knew she was in good hands. Then I asked her to describe what her two visitors looked like. Her description fitted that of the two Russians I'd got to know so well. I comforted her as best I could, saying that it was all right, the Embassy in Moscow would protect them, so she was not to worry.

I went home and tried to think things out. To me it was evident that they had attempted to recruit him too, and he had broken down under the strain. Whatever it was, by the time I had got home, I realised that I would have to do something other than just sit around and wait. Mrs Hall's mention of Watson had struck a chord in my memory. I knew John fairly well. Many years ago when I had first met him, it was whispered to me that besides being the manager of a Riga plywood mill, he was also a British secret service agent who had served in the First World War. It was not the thing in the British colony to speak or ask further questions about, you just accepted it. I decided I would make an attempt to contact him before it was too late.

We lived in a street called *Dainos Iela*, which was really only half a street. At the back of our house and at the end was a derelict building site. That evening I waited until after midnight and crept out of the flat along the corridor to the back window of the house which overlooked the building site and got out. Luckily, it was a thundery and overcast summer's night, and quite dark. Even now, I don't know how I managed to make that journey to Tornakalns, which was a suburb some two miles from where I lived, without being picked up by the night patrols. But make it I did.

It was about three a.m. when I reached the quiet suburb of Tornakalns where Watson lived. After some prolonged discreet tapping on the front windows the door was opened after I'd whispered through the letter box who I was.

'Christ Almighty man! What brings you here at this time of night?'

'I'm going to be shot so I thought I'd better see you first.'

He looked at me incredulously and then said, 'This calls for a drink. What'll you have?'

Over a couple of stiff whiskies I told him my story, beginning with the visit I had had from the two Russian so-called tobacco men, and my recent call on Glynn Hall. John said he knew about Glynn Hall's condition. He had, in fact, managed to get a permit for him and his wife to leave Latvia for Sweden, but on the way to the aerodrome Glynn had become unmanageable and had attempted to commit suicide by throwing himself out of the car. I then explained why I had not been around for fear of implicating other people in my troubles. I said that if he could somehow get a message through to Moscow about my plight, I'd be very grateful. I also added that in the event of my disappearance, would he keep an eye on my parents for me, and lastly, should any documents turn up incriminating me as a double agent and German spy, would he see that it was made known that they were forgeries. He told me not to worry. I did not stay long as I had to get back before daylight. On leaving he bade me keep a stiff upper lip and wished me the best of luck, promising that he would see to things for me.

I got home safely and felt that a great load had been lifted off my shoulders – my troubles were at last shared. I slept solidly for twelve hours – the first real sleep I'd had for months.

The next three weeks passed by without anything untoward happening. I made no further attempts to approach the authorities concerning my visas to leave the country. I knew it would be useless. I rarely went out and if I did, never went far from home. The news over the radio from England was far from heartening, but we were all convinced that everything would come out all right in the end and Churchill's broadcasts really bucked us up. How were things in Riga at this time? To me they seemed passably normal.

On the whole, food was still available, but gone was the superabundance; it was noticeable that all canned goods had disappeared and small queues were beginning to be evident in the shops. The services ran normally in Riga itself. Travelling by train was, however, very restricted. The streets had lost that bustle of humanity. Noticeable was the lack of younger men, where before one had seen young conscripts mingling among the populace, now there were none to be seen. Most of the cafés and restaurants were closed but some were still open and patronised by nondescript middle-aged people. The only time I saw younger people, was when they turned out in organised demonstration marches, and these were the workers. I often wondered what had happened to the tens of thousands or so of young military conscripts that had been under arms at the time of the Occupation.

The newspapers – the Lettish *Jaunakas Zinas* which was the largest and most popular one, the emigré Russian *Segodnya Vyecherom* still appeared but in a much reduced tabloid form. They now no longer dealt with the normal newsy topics, instead they were filled with articles extolling the might of the Soviet Union, the brotherly co-operation of the Lettish people, their security from war under Soviet protection, eulogies to Stalin; the constant achievements of the workers in industry and on the land. It was all so childishly written and repetitive that many papers lay in the kiosks unsold.

As I reviewed the hopelessness of my situation, the dominating fear of what would happen to my parents once the Russians had dealt with me, gave way to a bitter rage. That they would shoot me I had no doubt whatever, and I determined that when the time did come I would not be taken like the Letts I had seen, bundled helplessly into a truck to be carted away for slaughter, if I was going to die, then I'd take as many of my would-be executioners with me. I knew it was not their way to collect victims in broad daylight, this kind of work was left to special squads – lorry loads of armed soldiers at midnight.

I already had in my possession a small but deadly Belgium automatic pistol which I'd thought it wise to acquire whilst in Norway after the Nord Express incident. I decided to use this and made plans accordingly. My bedroom was at the end of the passage in the flat, so one evening after my parents had retired for the night I fixed up a photo flash in front of my bedroom door that would light up the passage for just a split second, it was all I needed. I then left the front door off the latch so that entry would present no obstacle, put out the lights and waited, half-concealed in the bedroom doorway. I reckoned that I could rake the passageway with at least one burst of fire aided by the flash which I hoped would put the soldiers off guard for a second or two. It would be all I required. I took up this vigil night after night, from the moment my mother and father retired until the hours of early dawn. Somehow I derived a feeling of grim satisfaction with the role I had adopted, even taking a flash picture of myself at the ready and fixing my camera so there could be one picture of the final scene when it transpired. As far as I was concerned it was to be 'Custer's Last Stand'. But it was not to be. The unexpected happened!

At ten a.m. on 19 October 1940, a car drew up outside our house. The man who stepped out and came into our flat was Henderson, the official interpreter to the British Embassy in Moscow. He informed me that Sir Stafford Cripps' private secretary, Geoffrey Wilson, together with another member of the Embassy had just arrived and were staying at the Rome Hotel. He had been sent to fetch me there. I was so relieved I could have wept. In next to no time I was in a room in the 'Rome' and being introduced. 'We hear you've been having trouble, Murray, tell us all about it and we'll draw up a statement which you'll sign,' were the first words addressed to me by Geoffrey Wilson.

I gave them a brief account of what had happened to me since the Soviet Occupation. It was written down whilst I recounted my experiences. I signed it, then Wilson said we would go to the Prefectura at once. On arriving there, we were immediately shown into the presence of the head of the Visas Department. I've always had a sense of humour and I really saw the funny side of the interview that took place. The official that we spoke to was Russian. Before he could say anything, Henderson adopted a bullying tone. Speaking in Russian, he said it was contrary to all regulations for a British subject, and member of His Britannic Majesty's Government to have been denied a visa to join his Embassy, and the Ambassador in Moscow would be compelled to make an official protest to the Kremlin. He mentioned nothing, however, about the incidents I had recounted. The Prefect we saw said he was sorry but the whole thing was due to a mistake on Mr Murray's part. He had certainly filled in the application forms, but had done so incorrectly, and furthermore Mr Murray did not need a visa but was free to travel to Moscow any time. All Mr Murray had to do was to submit his passport for stamping. In fact if he had it with him, the visas would be granted there and then. Henderson asked me, in English, to produce my passport, which I did, and it was taken off me and returned within a few minutes duly stamped with one all-embracing visa, both to leave Latvia and enter the Soviet Union via the Russian frontier town of Bigosova. It was also decided in conjunction with the officials that I leave Riga on the next train for Moscow, which would be the following day at four p.m.

We left the Prefectura and I was driven home. On the way I asked how it came about they'd come to Riga. Wilson said that actually they'd come to make arrangements for the evacuation of the British colony out of Latvia and the neighbouring states of Esthonia and Lithuania and that they would be staying on for a few days. I refrained from asking if they had known of my plight beforehand. Reaching home, Wilson said that I was not to worry, he'd be seeing me in Moscow, and that Henderson would be calling the following day to see me on to the train.

Arriving home, I told my mother the good news, explaining that it was through a mistake that my visa had been withheld, but now it was all right. That evening, when Dad came home, we sat quietly and talked of the future. I said that once in Moscow I would try and get them out of Latvia. They did not think it would be possible, but I said that one of the directors of my former Finnish firm, Sumer Limited, lived in Constantinople and that I would endeavour to get in touch with him to see if they could live in Constantinople. They both agreed that would be fine if I could arrange it. Then I said that if the postal service was normal between Riga and Moscow, I would write to them once a week and they could write to me. I pointed out that as sealed letters would be delayed by censorship, it would be best to write only on plain postcards, and only write to say how well things were going in Latvia. Should they be having any difficulties, they were to mention that 'the weather was bad', and I would understand and do something about it. They understood me.

Mother, as practical as ever, said, 'It will be cold in Moscow, you must get a good overcoat.' So I said that I would call in and see Mr Jakobson our family tailor and ask him if he could help me.

Early the next morning, I hurried off to see Elias Jakobson, owner of a large clothing business. He was an old friend of ours. When I had the cigarette factory, I used to make a special brand of cigarettes for him, imprinted with his name. When I reached the shop, he was serving behind the counter. 'Look, it has come to this, times have changed,' he sadly remarked. He explained that his business now no longer belonged to him but was in the hands of the works committee who had allowed him to stay on as a counter-hand. Most of his business was now making things for the Russians and their families who were arriving in Latvia, and it was for this reason they were allowed to obtain further stocks of tex-tiles. I told him I was leaving for Moscow and would need a warm winter coat. He disappeared into a back room and came out bearing a beautifully-made padded black coat with a large beaver skin fur collar. 'I made this for myself,' he said, 'you take it, I don't think I'll be needing it now.' He absolutely refused to take the full value of the coat, so I paid him a nominal sum which was duly entered on my passport – in accordance with the newly-passed sales regu-lations. The coat was to give me good service throughout the time I was in Russia. As he was the same build as myself, it was a perfect fit. When I brought it home, my parents were cheered up by it.

Henderson called for me later that afternoon, and after saying goodbye to Dad and Mam we drove off to the station. Henderson saw me on to the train. I had practically a whole coach to myself, and the five or six Russian officers who shared the coach had separate compartments. It was about five p.m. as the train steamed out of the station. There seemed to be more goods wagons than passenger coaches to the train. At about midnight, we arrived at the frontier station of Bigosova and a porter appeared and motioned me to get out on to the platform. It was a miserable deserted station and consisted of a long wooden building dividing the two main tracks with wooden roofing jutting out over the platforms. My baggage and passport were collected from me, and I was by pantomime gestures, given to understand that I was to remain where I was until called for. I was not allowed to be present at the examination of my suitcases of which I had three. It was a wet, chilly October night, and I must have paced up and down smoking innumerable cigarettes for nearly two hours. There was no buffet and not even a waiting room. The lighting must have consisted of forty-watt bulbs it was so murky and dark. In the end, the porter approached and led me to the other platform where a second train was standing.

The coach I was conducted to was a big roomy, luxurious affair. My compartment had carpet and curtains; an upper bunk with clean sheets and blankets already prepared; and there was much gleaming solid brasswork evident. A small door at the side led to a sumptuously-appointed washroom with toilet. The woodwork was of richly-hued mahogany. I surmised that it was a luxury coach from the old Tsarist times, the furnishings and fittings being so obviously old-fashioned. A sliding door led into the corridor and soon the conductor appeared carrying my baggage. Having deposited my luggage, he went away and shortly returned with my passport and what was most welcome, a glass of hot pale tea with a slice of lemon floating on top. I had no money, but offered him a couple of packets of cigarettes which he accepted gratefully with a smile.

This coach, like the other, did not carry many passengers. The same officers, augmented by three or four more, were the only other travellers. They seemed to be picked from a special branch. Dressed similarly in smart uniforms and top boots, they stood about six foot, and must have weighed in the region of two hundred pounds. All were clean-shaven with close cropped hair. They made no attempt to speak to me as they passed the door of my compartment at intervals.

I was naturally very curious to see what Russia was like, but it was hopeless trying to peer through the double-glazed windows. There was only inky blackness outside which accentuated the reflection of the interior of my compartment like an impenetrable mirror. My mother had packed me a nice selection of sandwiches and after munching some of them, I turned in and went to sleep. This was not difficult. The comforting warmth of the coach and the steady rolling motion of the carriage, soon lulled me off into quite a deep sleep. It was eleven o'clock the next morning when the conductor woke me up with a welcome glass of tea and lemon, which was terrifically refreshing. It is amazing how dry and parched one's throat and mouth become when travelling all night in a train. I got up, washed, dressed myself and once again concentrated on having a look at the country through which I was travelling. So this is Russia! I thought as I gazed through the window.

The weather was grey and drizzly. For long periods we passed through thick pine forests, and when we emerged into the open there was nothing but vast expanses of uncultivated land with here and there an occasional homestead to be seen. I never caught a glimpse of either cattle, sheep or horses. To me it looked a strange, forbidding, desolate sort of country. As the hours passed by, we did stop at a number of stations – weather-beaten wooden shacks, all unpainted and sadly in need of repair. There were no towns or even villages surrounding them. They looked as though they had been planted indiscriminately in the deserted countryside. Huddled in groups along the platforms were groups of peasants and working people. It was difficult to tell the men from the women, except the women had kerchiefs drawn tightly round their faces. They were all clad in dirty and greasy, padded three-quarter-length coats. They wore knee-length thick felt boots with rubber over-shoes. They seemed to wear all their wardrobe on their backs, their appearance was so fat and cumbersome. All had bundles tied up in cloth with bits of rope and straps. I did not observe one suitcase among them. As the train stopped, there was inevitably a free-for-all scramble to board the train and much shouting and pandemonium; none, however, approached the coach I was in – it was avoided like the plague! The same scene was repeated whenever we stopped at a station. The hours soon passed by and darkness fell at about four in the afternoon.

It must have been ten o'clock that night when the train finally steamed into Moscow's Baltic Station. At least this station was properly lit up and I peered anxiously through the window, wondering who would be there to meet me.

Part IV

The Spy called Swallow

The train stopped. It was hard to believe that I was at last in Moscow. Through the window I could see crowds of people swarming around the passengers alighting from the coaches at the further end of the train. The fact that there was an empty space in front of my coach, except for one of the NKVD officers who stood around, made the contrast very noticeable. Then, through the barrier opposite, two figures approached. To my surprise, I recognised one as Mr Bagshawe who I had met on a couple of occasions in Helsinki. He was the Secretary to the Naval Attaché in Moscow and sometimes came to Finland with the diplomatic bag on courier duty. The small sallow-faced man standing by his side was unknown to me.

'Hello, Murray, so you've arrived at last!' was his greeting as I alighted. 'This is Shura, my chauffeur. I've got the car outside. We'll drive home to my place.'

We were soon driving along in an old Hillman Minx that coughed and spluttered frequently and seemed to run in starts and jerks, but it was comfortable and roomy enough inside. Bagshawe was proud of it. He told me he had bought it for a hundred pounds from one of the newspaper correspondents who had had to leave Russia.

It did not take more than ten minutes to reach his place. We drew up to the gates of a fairly large house set in its own grounds surrounded by a high brick wall. Inside the gates stood a lodge out of which emerged a porter to open the gates.

'That's Vasily,' Bagshawe remarked. 'He's the porter, stoker, gardener and what-have-you for the place.'

When we got inside the house, he showed me round and

pointed out that his flat consisted of three bedrooms, a large sitting room, dining room, and kitchen, and an adjoining bedroom which was occupied by the housekeeper, Rebecca, to whom he introduced me. She was a small Jewish woman of indeterminate age, sad-eyed with greying hair that had once been black. He said he also had a cook, Valentina, who lived out but came in daily to do the necessary shopping and prepare the meals. He introduced me to her the next morning. She was a fat, jolly woman, and I found out later, a very good cook indeed, whose culinary efforts though lost on Bagshawe, really roused the envy of our not-so-fortunate guests at the parties we gave.

He explained that the building was composed of several self-contained flats. There was another ground floor flat and this was occupied by the Embassy archivist who lived there with his French wife. There were also two top floor flats, one of which was occupied by a Mr Scott and his Russian wife. Scott was the clerk to the Commercial Attaché. The other flat belonged to Colonel Greer who did not live in it but had all his personal furniture stored there. It was a lovely building and Bagshawe told me that it had been the former Finnish Embassy, and the name of the street we were in was called *Maly kharitonevsky*.

The first thing I did was to have a quick bath. After that I joined Bagshawe for a light supper of cold meat and pickles, with a couple of small glasses of Vodka. I was astonished at Bagshawe's capacity for it. He drank it as though it was water and seemed none the worse for it. During the meal he explained that there was a flat for me in a street called *Petrovka* which was some distance away. It was a tenement house and the other flats were occupied by Russian families and I could take it if I wished. My predecessor, who had been sent home for reasons of health, had formerly lived there, but should I be agreeable I could share this flat with him and also share the expenses which would turn out cheaper for me. I told Bagshawe that it was okay with me and that I'd prefer to share his place and would inform my chief accordingly.

At nine o'clock the next morning we drove to the Embassy. A large imposing building in the *Sofiyskaya naberezhnaya* which stood on the banks of a wide canal separating it from the massive walls of the Kremlin, above which could be seen the onion-shaped domes of innumerable churches. To me it looked like a scene from the Arabian Nights.

We drove through the gates of the drive leading to the Embassy entrance, armed sentries stood on both sides.

When we left our house, I'd noticed two cars, each containing two occupants in civilian clothes, standing opposite the house. One of the cars had immediately started up and tailed us as far as the Embassy where it pulled up at the side of the railings and joined a further line of cars standing there. Bagshawe's comment to my enquiry was, 'Oh, they are the YMCA, you'll soon get used to them following you around!' It appeared that the 'YMCA' was the humorous appellative bestowed upon the NKVD by the Embassy staff.

Inside the Embassy, I was first introduced to my future chief, Wing-Commander Hallawell, the Air Attaché, then to Captain Clanchy, Bagshawe's boss and afterwards to Colonel Greer, Military Attaché and his secretary, Jimes. The three services thus represented had their offices on the western side of the building.

After the introductions were over, my chief said it was time to keep the appointment he had made for me with the Ambassador, Sir Stafford Cripps. We went to his private study. In the room, already seated, were the two other attachés, Geoffrey Wilson, whom I'd met in Riga, and Mr Dunlop, senior secretary to the Embassy, as well as Mr James, the senior stenographer. After the introductory formalities were over, Sir Stafford, who was just like the pictures I'd seen of him, tall, thin, sharp-featured, wearing glasses, gave me a somewhat wintry smile and said, 'Well, it's nice to see you Murray. From what I can gather you seem to have had some difficulty in getting here. Perhaps you'd like to tell us about it. Take your time and tell us exactly what happened.'

They listened in silence as I recounted the incident of those nightmarish four months I had spent in Riga. When I had finished, Sir Stafford asked, 'Are you prepared to swear that the account you have given us is the truth, and sign a statement to that effect?'

'Certainly, Sir,' I answered.

He rose and came over to me. 'That is all, we shall prepare your statement for signature, but before you go, I should like to tell you that we have been aware that in the past, certain members of our staff have, from time to time, been intimidated by Soviet agents. You are the first one so far that has had the courage to come forward and report the fact. Thank you, Murray.'

The next day I was told to report to Sir Stafford, who handed me a typewritten copy of the statement I had made the previous day.

'Read it very carefully, Murray, and let me know if there is any point on which you disagree.' It was perfect, and I signed it there and then. He asked me if I was still worried about my parents and I answered, 'Very much so!'

'I have been thinking about them also,' he told me, and went on to explain that on behalf of the Government he was going to send a very strong protest to Vyshinsky, of the Soviet Foreign Ministry, about the treatment one of his staff had been subjected to by the Soviet Secret Police, pointing out that they had used the threat of taking action against his parents in order to force him to acquiesce to their demands. He surmised that following this, it was quite unlikely the Russians would take any steps to harm my parents, as they would certainly deny the charges the British Government brought against them, and would make sure nothing happened to my parents in order to prove their point. This seemed a reasonable assumption to me also. He asked me if I had any plans with regard to them. I said that I had business friends in Istanbul who would look after them if only I could make contact with Turkey and get them out of Russia.

'In that case,' he said, 'you can forward a letter by the next diplomatic bag going to Istanbul.'

At the end of my meeting with the Ambassador, he mentioned that he would very much like me to have tea with Lady Cripps and himself if I would care to come. I said I would be delighted. The next day I received an invitation signed by Lady Cripps.

It was quite an informal tea-party. Both his daughters, Peggy and Theresa, were present and they made me feel very much at home. Lady Cripps asked me if I would contribute to the Prisoners of War Fund she was organising and I said I would be only too pleased to, considering that I had very nearly been one myself. She asked me how that had come about, so I related my experiences in Norway. Sir Stafford also told me that Mr Lascelles was also now one of his secretaries in the Embassy which was news to me, as I had last seen him in Sweden and did not know he had come to Moscow.

The next two days I spent in Bagshawe's flat sorting out my things and making myself at home so to speak. The arrangements I had made with Bagshawe suited me admirably and I was able to settle up with him for my share of the food store, wines and spirits, etc. that he already had in stock, which financially was of very great help to him.

I had already sent an open card to my parents telling them I had arrived safe and sound, that Russia and the people were marvellous and that I hoped they were keeping well.

The first task I undertook in my new appointment was to learn the combination of the Wing-Commander's safe. Under his watchful eye, I spent some time manipulating the combination until I was word perfect, as one might say. It took some effort on my part as I always was, and still am, pretty dim where remembering figures is concerned. Then we had a long talk about the scope of my duties, but the most important were the 'don'ts'!

We understood one another well, and I couldn't have wished for a better chief. Beyond saying that I typed out all his confidential reports and in conjunction with the other two services' secretaries did the deciphering and coding of messages to the respective service branches of the Foreign Office, I will say no more.

We three service departments – Naval, Military and Air Force, were pretty well occupied with work. Although it was all new to me, I quickly acquired the necessary knowledge, and I had the edge over my colleagues as I could both type pretty fast and take dictation in shorthand.

Captain Clanchy, as befitted the Chief of the Senior Service, kept up what appeared to me a quaint and pleasing custom, but my colleagues, Bagshawe and Jimes always made fun of it. Each morning before we commenced our duties, we would assemble in his office and he would take out a decanter of sherry from his cupboard with four glasses, hand a small wine glass to each of us, fill them up with sherry and we would drink a toast, 'To His Majesty, the King!' I always felt sorry for Bagshawe on these occasions – he could only stomach spirits and the sherry used to half choke him, but with his chief's eye fixed sternly upon him, he had to down it!

The second week after my arrival Bagshawe said it was time for us to throw a party so that I could be introduced to the rest of the 'Lower Deck' diplomatic circle, as he put it. As the social life in Moscow revolved round such parties, members of the British and American Embassies each gave parties in turn at the slightest excuse, it was the only means of relieving the tension of living in Moscow under constant and hostile supervision. Several members of the American Embassy turned up that evening among whom was Reinhardt, the cipher officer I had met in Riga. He asked me why I had been so long in getting to Moscow. I said it was due to visa difficulties, which surprised him, as he said he had had no trouble with his and reckoned it was because the Americans commanded more respect than we did.

Amongst others who turned up for the party were three very well known newspaper correspondents. Walter Durante, who I'd already met in Stockholm and who had come to Moscow hoping to obtain another interview with Stalin; Henry Shapiro who represented Associated Press, and Monsieur Champignon of *Le Temps*. He, in a way, was the odd man out and his quiet manner betokened the strain he was living under at the time. France having fallen to the Germans, it was a question of whether he represented the Pétain Government or the Free French. Then he had also the problem of where his money was to come from and whether the Soviet government would allow him to remain in Russia. When members of the Press became *persona non grata* the time granted for departure from Russia was generally limited to hours, with no nonsense allowed. I really sympathised with his predicament. Although it was an Embassy instruction that we were not to fraternise with the Press you could never keep journalists out once they'd got wind of a party. On the whole, they were a good lot and as far as my experience went, they never tried anything on, either with regard to getting messages passed through the censorship or pumping me for inside information.

The party had just got under way when I was surprised to see three more guests turn up. My surprise was due to the fact that they were young Russian girls. Two of them seemed to be well known to two of our Embassy staff. They were introduced all round, and there was much laughing and gesticulating as none of them spoke English. It was the third girl that attracted my attention however. Bagshawe explained to me that he had met her in the Hotel Metropole some weeks ago and having had already a party in mind had thought it a good idea to invite her along. During the introductions I found she could speak German and that her name was Nora. In contrast to the other girls who soon made themselves at home, she seemed very shy and reserved. The others were heavily made-up and drank and smoked a lot. She, on the other hand, wore no make-up at all and neither drank nor smoked. With her fair hair and complexion, large grey-green eyes and high cheek bones, she looked a typical Russian. She seemed much younger than the other two, about twenty-one, I surmised. I did not speak to her again after being introduced and when the three girls left shortly before midnight, I only felt curious as to how they came to be allowed to have contact with people like ourselves. Every report I had read on Russia, emphasised the fact that their civilians were neither allowed to mix or speak with foreigners unless supervised and that the secret police, who were everywhere and very much feared, made sure of this.

The party lasted until the late hours of the morning. I am not a teetotaller and will drink for company's sake, but I always drank very sparingly. When I first arrived in Latvia, I went to a party where I'd been given Vodka and then wine. I was violently sick and very ill for several days afterwards. It was a lesson to me in drinking that I never forgot. Vodka and wine do not mix and if you drink, it's better to stick to the one drink throughout the evening, and leave the hardened topers to drink spirits and follow them up with chasers. I spent most of the time talking to Champignon who also was not much of a spirit drinker and only drank wine. He seemed more knowledgeable than the others about life in Moscow and I was anxious to learn as much as I could. I asked if he knew the fair girl that had just left and he said he'd not seen her before at any of the parties and she was probably a new 'mozhno' girl. 'Mozhno girls,' he explained, meant 'permitted girls'; girls who were permitted by the secret police to fraternise with foreigners. Normally, as I have said, Russian citizens steered clear of foreigners. They were constantly exhorted through press and radio media to beware of foreigners who were all classed as agents, provocateurs and spies endangering the safety of the Soviet Union. The penalties for transgression were so swiftly and silently carried out and moreover, could bring such a wide circle of relations and friends under suspicion, that people were terrified even to speak to foreigners. Those that were involved with them in an official capacity even, never seemed to last long. The dapper Vladimir Barkoff, the Soviet Chief of Protocol whom I saw several times in the Embassy, was one of these. They ultimately disappeared at some time or other and any enquiries made met with vague and inconclusive replies. The mozhno girls, on the other hand, were not employed or paid by the State, they were just left to their own devices, but they had to give constant reports on their foreign contacts. These, too, as soon as they could serve no further useful purpose or in any way became embarrassing to the State, were silently disposed of and disappeared without any trace.

Champignon told me an amusing story about one of the former French diplomats who was having a steady affair with one of the mozhno girls. One day his car was stopped on a country road and he was approached by a couple of NKVD agents who had been tailing him. In the course of the ensuing conversation he was asked if he would like to work for the Soviet Union. When he indignantly refused, one of them produced a packet of photographs of intimate bedroom scenes portraying him in a series of very compromising positions with his Russian girl friend. These, he was informed, would be sent to the Embassy if he did not co-operate with them. He took one look at their photos, pulled out his wallet, and took out some photographs of his own. 'Phooey!' he said, 'that's nothing. Here! Look at these! Your people can't take photographs for nuts! Go on, take these, tell your bosses they can have them with my compliments!' He happened to be an expert photographer and had taken pictures of himself with the same girl in such an astounding variety of sexual postures, that even the Russians were astonished. After this they left him alone and the story caused immense amusement when it got around the diplomatic circles. The only sad part about the whole affair was that he never saw his girl friend again.

The weeks passed swiftly by as I gradually worked myself into the Embassy routine, but most annoyingly, I kept receiving telephone calls from Nora, the girl I met at the party, who was always asking me to go out with her. The fact that our telephone number was ex-directory and could not be obtained by people other than Embassy staff, was suspicious. Again, she always called when I was alone in the house – a fact she seemed to be aware of. When she rang I cut her off quickly as soon as I knew it was her, but she never took no for an answer.

The Christmas of 1940 arrived and the unusual procedure adopted by Sir Stafford Cripps for its celebration caused a few raised eyebrows in the Embassy. It also shed light on the character of the man. He invited the whole staff to a Christmas dinner held in the official Embassy reception hall. The invitation sent out stated that ordinary lounge suits should be worn to avoid embarrassment to those members who did not possess dinner jackets, and that seating arrangements would be decided by guests drawing lots instead of sitting at the table in accordance to precedence of rank. This gave the Embassy staff a chance of meeting each other socially on common ground.

The Christmas party was quite a success as far as I was concerned and Lady Cripps had done everything possible to make it so: we had turkey, goose and pork, with traditional Christmas pudding and mince pies, and plenty of beer, wine and spirits.

After Christmas a series of irritating incidents occurred. Bagshawe had gone out for the evening and I was alone in the house reading when the telephone rang.

'Who's speaking?' I asked.

'Is that Meester John? It's me, Nora. You remember me don't you?' came the reply in German.

I was angry at being disturbed and one thing I didn't want, was to start getting entangled with a Russian mozhno girl. I answered her back in the snappiest tone I could adopt.

'Yes I remember you, and this is Mr Murray speaking. What do you want?'

'I want to speak to you and . . .'

I cut her off short. 'But I don't want to speak to you, and I'm very busy! Goodbye!'

With that I hung up the receiver and went back to my book, feeling very satisfied that I'd nipped the unwelcome intrusion in the bud.

Half an hour later the 'phone rang again. I bet it's that damn girl again, I thought. Sure enough, I was right. I did not give her the chance to get properly started.

'Look here Miss Nora, will you please understand I do not wish to speak or hear from you at all! Is that understood?' and with that I banged the receiver down.

I was not disturbed again that night and I did not mention the matter to Bagshawe.

Two nights later however, when I was again alone in the house, the 'phone rang again. It was Nora.

'Can I meet you somewhere, Mr Murray? I'd like to talk to you.'

I was really angry this time. 'Miss Nora,' I spoke deliberately, 'I've told you before, I don't want to have anything to do with you. Please leave me alone and stop ringing me up!' With that I slammed the phone down.

I was not disturbed again until New Year's Eve which brought with it a dilemma that was to have an unexpected and shattering effect upon my stay in Russia.

Bagshawe had gone to a New Year's Eve party, I, having refused the invitation, remained alone in the flat. I'd just settled myself down comfortably when I was interrupted by the sound of the telephone ringing. I picked up the receiver — it was Nora! I shouted, 'Not at home!' and replaced the receiver. The bell rang again in a long incessant tone. Determined to put a stop to this situation once and for all, I picked up the receiver.

'Mr Murray, I must speak to you, I must, I must,' Nora's voice ended in a wail. I could almost see the tears as her voice ended in a sob.

'All right then come round, but I can't spare much time.'

There was a muffled sob and a click as she rang off. Within a matter of minutes the doorbell rang. I opened the door myself as Rebecca had long since gone to bed.

It was Nora and she gave me a nervous hesitant smile as I led her into the sitting room and told her to be seated. I had already made up my mind how to handle the situation and wasted no time. I adopted a bullying tone. 'Look here, Nora, you've been bothering me now for a long time. It's got to stop! You understand?' I spoke contemptuously. 'I know you are a mozhno girl sent to spy on me, but you'll get nothing out of me and I don't want to know you or have anything to do with you, so go back to your secret police and tell them I've said so. You ought to be ashamed of yourself – a young girl like you carrying on in this way! Now please go.'

It was a long-winded effort, but I'd got it off my chest at last. Naturally, I expected some sort of vehement denial, but the effect was totally unexpected. As I stood over her, she looked up at me. Her eyes widened like big grey-green saucers. Her lips began to quiver. In that instant her expression changed. I glimpsed the face of a young girl suddenly confronted with the realisation that the whole world was tumbling about her. She had the look of an animal beaten beyond endurance. With a long drawn out 'O——— oh!' she put her hands to her face and sobbed as though her heart was breaking. I let her alone, waiting until the paroxysm should end, wondering meanwhile whether or not her grief was genuine. I could, however, not forget the look of utter hopelessness on her face just before she broke down. I stared at her – and as I looked down, I saw before me the face of a child, torn with unutterable grief and terror. For a fleeting moment I felt a strange feeling of pity and compassion for the girl in front of me. Again, her eyes had the look of a stricken animal that had been badly hurt – although she was looking at me, her eyes seemed to look beyond and through me. I felt strangely troubled. Leaving her, I went to the kitchen and made a strong pot of tea. I poured out a couple of cups, added milk, and sweetened them well and gave her one. She looked up at me dumbly.

'Here, have a nice cup of English tea, it will do you good,' I said in a coaxing tone. She took it and began to sip it mechanically.

'Now, tell me who you really are, and what your name is?'

My change of tone and manner began to bring her back to life and she gave me a timid smile.

'Go on,' I coaxed. 'Tell me everything about yourself. Where are your mother and father, and where do you live?'

'I have no mother. She is dead and my father is in prison.' She burst out crying again. I let her cry and waited patiently until her sobs had subsided, and repeated gently, 'Go on, tell me, don't be frightened, there is nothing to be afraid of.'

She began to talk, on and on she went and as her story unfolded I could not but help feeling a mounting wave of pity for the plight she was in.

Her full name it appeared was Nina Nora Vasilievna Korzhenko. She had been born in Zolotonosha, a suburb of Poltava in the Ukraine. Her mother had committed suicide when Nora was only seven years old. Her memory of her mother was that of a loving kindly woman who had treated her with all the affection and tenderness a mother could bestow upon an only child.

Her father was Major Vasily Korzhenko of the Soviet Security Force, the GPU, the precursor of the present day NKVD. He had a brother, her uncle Konstantin who lived in Leningrad and had formerly been a colonel in the Tsarist Army. Her father and his brother often quarrelled but still had a great affection for one another. Her uncle was an eminent engineer and for that reason his life had been spared by the Bolsheviks, apart from the fact that his brother Vasily used his influence to get him out of the frequent troubles caused by Konstantin's outspoken criticism of the Bolsheviks.

It was during one of her father's interrogations of 'Enemies of the State' that he met the wife of a suspected German national and fell in love with her. The shock of his unfaithfulness had so preyed on the mind of Nora's mother that she poisoned herself and took her own life. Her father later married his new-found love Ursula and before long a son was born to them and called Felix, so she now had a step-brother. After this, Ursula's mother came to join them and the whole family moved to Moscow, Major Korzhenko having been promoted to a special appointment in the Foreign Ministry. Nora by this time had grown up and was studying for entrance to Moscow University, of which she was now a student.

All had been going well when, without warning her father was suddenly arrested and committed to the notorious Lubyanka prison.

Before the distraught family could get over this tragedy, her stepmother Ursula was also arrested in the middle of the night and exiled to Tashkent in Asiatic Russia. All this was at the time of the great purges in 1939 following Molotov's appointment as Foreign Secretary. In spite of these events, her grandmother managed to take care of little Felix and Nora herself continued with her studies for the University.

It was one morning in the April of 1940 that she observed an elderly man who turned out to be a Hungarian diplomat experiencing some difficulty in making himself understood in the Moscow main post office. He could only speak German other than Hungarian which the post office staff could not understand so Nora interpreted for him. He was very grateful and asked her if she would guide him around Moscow as he was a complete stranger. She did so.

Some days after this incident, as she sat alone in her study room preparing her paper for the next morning's lecture, there came a sudden knock on the door. Opening it she was startled to see two men in civilian clothes who brushed her aside as they walked in. They informed her that they were from the secret police and requested her to get ready and accompany them at once to their headquarters. She was too terrified to say or do anything but comply with their command. They drove her to the Hotel Metropole where, in an upstairs suite she was brought before a Major Kirilov, one of the heads of the Soviet espionage departments. Bewildered and frightened, she listened as she was angrily accused of consorting with a foreigner who was an enemy of the state, the punishment for which would be severe. The Major then altered his tone and said he knew all about her and her family. If she really was a good citizeness of the Soviet and prepared to help her father who was still in prison and alive, she could prove it by working for his department against the enemies of Russia. The thought of at last being able to do something to help her father, about whom she had been unable to get any information whatsoever, made her only too anxious to accept the offer. She was then told that she would work under the pseudonym of 'The Swallow' and from thence onwards she was only to communicate with them under that name. After being given precise instructions as to her duties, which included permission to frequent the restaurant of the Hotel Metropole and contact foreign guests, she was made aware of the dire penalties that would be imposed upon her for betrayal or failure. Following this she was allowed to go home.

It was after this that one evening late in September she had met Bagshawe at the Metropole Hotel, and he had asked her to dance with him. During the course of that evening he mentioned to her that he would be shortly giving a party to celebrate the arrival of a new member of the British Embassy and he invited her to come to it.

This news she had passed on to Major Kirilov who had immediately summoned her to his presence.

She was showered with congratulations on her success. The Major then handed her a dossier. The first thing she saw was a photograph of myself with pages of written material which she was not allowed to read.

'This is the man you will meet at the party,' he said. 'He is not just a secretary but a dangerous British agent who is an armament and aerodynamics specialist. It will be your duty to contact him and use every means possible to gain his confidence. It is up to you. Do you understand?' He then warned her that under no circumstances was she to say or ask anything that would arouse my suspicions, as it would be for his department to take care of me once she had achieved her objective.

As she finished her narrative I looked closely at her. She reminded me more than ever of some poor animal that had been caught in a trap. Instinctively, I knew that basically what she had told me was the truth about herself. But I wanted to know more.

As she stopped she looked up at me. 'Well,' I remarked, 'go on.'

'But you would not meet me or even talk to me and the Major has said he will give me one more chance and if I fail, I will be put away. What shall I do? What is going to happen to my father now . . . ?' Her voice tailed off into a hopeless cry.

I was in a dilemma. The proper course of action was for me to inform the Embassy of the incident. This, I figured, would result in two things. First, the girl before me would suffer; secondly, the Secret Police who it seemed were out to get me would resort to other means of pressurising me. As my parents were still in their power, they might even wreak their revenge on them, for the second rebuff that they had received at my expense.

The other alternative open to me was to play along with the girl and use her as a cat's paw in getting my parents out of Latvia, which

86

was a chance I would have to take. I made a decision. I decided to tell her that I would meet her occasionally and if it came to demands for information, I would concoct trivia to keep her bosses happy for as long as it suited my purpose.

She had been watching me closely whilst I was turning all this over in my mind. I smiled at her, and said, 'Good. I will meet you sometimes Miss Korzhenko, but I am a very busy man and will not be able to see you often. So now, go home and report to your Major that you have at last made an appointment with me.'

'What do you mean?' she asked wonderingly.

'I'll tell you what I mean, you'll come here twice a week to give me Russian lessons, and you will come at eight o'clock until nine o'clock in the morning, because at that time everybody will be about in the house and it will look less suspicious than in the evenings when the flat is sometimes empty.'

As I finished, she did something that caused me no little embarrassment. She caught hold of my hands, drew them to her lips and kissed them. Tears ran down her cheeks as she murmured, 'Oh, thank you Mr Murray! Thank you.' I felt a bit of a hypocrite, but thought that anyway I was helping her as well, which was some consolation for making use of her.

Although throughout our conversation we spoke in German, she used the appellation Mister not Herr, so I said she was to call me John from now on. I then told her to listen very carefully to what I had to say. I spoke very slowly to make sure that she understood. I said I would trust her to be a faithful and honest friend, but as my life would depend on it, she, for her part, must trust me implicitly and I would try to help her. I impressed upon her that if the Embassy knew we were friends, it would be the end of everything, and that it was most important she kept me informed what Major Kirilov or any of his staff said, or instructed her to carry out, as this was the only way that I could make plans for her to keep her bosses satisfied with her work for them. She said she understood and swore that she would never betray our trust. By this time it was already the early hours of the morning so I told her she had better go and when she reported to Major Kirilov, she was only to say that we had a pleasant meeting and that she had finally persuaded me to employ her to teach me Russian.

It was a much happier girl that I escorted out from the gates of the house that early New Year's Day morning, and I smiled too, as after she had gone down the street, a waiting car standing outside the house pulled away from the kerb and followed her.

I knew Bagshawe would not return until the morning, for a party was a party to him, and as there was always unlimited booze I knew he would remain right until the bitter end.

I turned in and spent a restless few hours getting to sleep, my mind busy with niggling problems, doubtful as to whether I really could trust the girl who had just left. At all costs I had to keep the Embassy out of it, at this stage anyway.

Bagshawe came home at midday and I mentioned that I'd had a visitor the night before and that it was the Russian girl who had been at our party, and that she had promised to give me Russian lessons a couple of times a week. His only reaction was to turn to me with a twinkle in his eye and say, 'That'll keep you out of mischief, but be careful my lad, you know what she is!' and there the matter ended.

Three days later Nora 'phoned and said she would be coming to give me my first lesson.

The morning she arrived, I took the precaution of introducing her to the staff and we had breakfast together for the benefit of my first Russian lesson. After it was over, I escorted her to the gate and on the way, out of earshot of everyone, she told me what had transpired on reporting to her chief, Major Kirilov. He had been tremendously pleased and had congratulated her upon her success. He had told her she was to do everything to ripen our friendship and reiterated that under no circumstances was she to ask me any questions about my work, or say anything that would alarm me. She was to charge me well for the 'Russian lessons'. She had nothing else to do, but just that, when the time came, it would be he and his staff who would take me in hand. For the time being she was only to work hard to gain my trust and confidence in any manner possible, which shouldn't be difficult for a pretty girl like her.

I could only smile. The weeks, then months, went by. Occasionally on a Saturday or Sunday I would go out openly in the daytime for a walk with Nora and she would show me around

Moscow, which has a charm of its own in winter. I was used to the cold. It was a dry, clean, fresh cold. We'd go on the Metro Underground, of which the Russians were very proud and rightly so, it was kept so clean and tidy. But my favourite spot was the Sokolniki Park which was an ideal place for freedom of conversation. It had one advantage, one could walk there and if we were followed, our followers were easily discernible. Nora had by now lost that frightened appearance and was beginning to look quite bright and cheery. It was on one of these occasions that I told her, should she by any chance have any trouble at any time and could not come to my home, she was to telephone me or get a message to me simply saying she would see me in the Park and I would meet her here in the Sokolniki, not that I thought there would be any trouble for her. After some weeks had elapsed, her Russian masters got impatient and began to press her to make arrangements for me to meet one of their staff. I fobbed this off with an explanation that I was being watched by my own Embassy. To sweeten the pill of disappointment I gave her certain 'information' to pass on. I compiled this information from a detailed study I made of the Russian newspapers we were supplied within the Embassy, together with items that were openly broadcast on the radio from England. I embroidered this information with highly complimentary bits about the size and power of the Soviet air force that was being talked about among the diplomatic staff. As I strung it out and Nora passed it on, she got gratified acclaims of approval from the NKVD. I spent a great deal of time and ingenuity in formulating these so-called reports.

One night as I sat up late doing my Russian homework, I decided to go into the kitchen for a glass of milk. As it was so quiet I became aware of a strange shuffling noise coming from Rebecca's room which adjoined the kitchen. Now Rebecca was a strange woman. She would carry out her duties silently and a 'good-morning' and a 'good-night' was the most one would get from her, although she spoke English like a native. This shuffling noise disturbed me; even when I went back to read it was annoyingly audible. As it was getting on my nerves, I went back to the kitchen, deciding to peep through the keyhole of her door to see if it was anything serious. As I looked I could make out Rebecca trudging round and round the small table in her room. Her head was sunk on her breast, her hands tightly clasped behind her. She did not walk – she just shuffled along; her eyes downcast, staring at the floor. I went back to my room wondering.

The next morning when talking to Bagshawe, I said I'd heard a strange shuffling noise coming from the kitchen. He replied, 'Oh, that's Rebecca. You needn't let that worry you,' and went on to give me the history of Rebecca as he knew it. She had been brought to England from Russia by her aunt during the Bolshevik Revolution, she grew up there and later worked in a bank in London. Misled by the glowing reports advertised by the Soviet Intourist Bureau, she decided, as she was now a British citizen, it would be safe for her to travel to Russia and meet all the relatives she had never seen. She arrived in Russia during the early thirties, and went to Minsk. Her relatives, frightened by her arrival, disowned her. She was arrested by the Secret Police, her passport and papers confiscated, and sentenced without trial to five years' imprisonment. In vain she protested that she was a British subject. They said that she was a Russian and as such, subject to Soviet law. She served her time – God knows how she survived, but survive she did. After her release, she managed to contact the British Embassy who tried to help her. But, as according to Soviet law, she was still a Soviet citizen, the most her Embassy could do was to persuade the authorities to allow her to work for them, and so she was given the job of housekeeper in *Maly kharitonevsky*. Bagshawe said that whenever she was upset, her mind reverted to her prison experiences, and she would walk round and round the table in her room as she used to do for exercise during her term of imprisonment. I was deeply moved by this story, and put myself out to be extra kind to her.

At this time there was one thing that did much to alleviate the apprehension I felt over the safety of my parents. Up to the time of meeting Nora, I had regularly written them a postcard, as agreed, every fortnight. I never had a reply. Later I was to learn that they did in fact receive my cards and replied immediately, but their replies never came through. But it was not long after taking Nora on as my Russian teacher I began to receive postcards regularly from Riga addressed to the Embassy saying that all was well. This was a great relief, but it also confirmed my suspicion that the NKVD were adept in the use of psychology to gain their objectives. Why they were still so interested in recruiting my services I could not fathom. I could not understand how they came to classify me as a dangerous agent. I was, however, glad that I'd befriended Nora even if I did not trust her entirely. I felt that I could handle the situation and my only fear, which was a valid one, was the Embassy. I did not want them on my back at this stage, because they would certainly not understand or condone my actions and it was for this reason I made sure that my acquaintance with Nora could not be misconstrued. She herself must have often been puzzled by the brusqueness of my manner at times.

I was very curious to see the Hotel Metropole, which I now knew to be one of the centres of Russian espionage and got Bagshawe to accompany me there on several occasions. He was quite happy to take me and it broke the monotony of some of our evenings. I'd treat him to a bottle of Vodka and generally had half a bottle of Russian wine myself, which I found extremely good. It was quite an impressive building, situated on the corner of Sverdlov Square, based on an imposing red granite podium which accentuated the simple smooth white plastered walls of its upper four storeys. It had actually been designed by the British architect, W. Walcott in 1899.

The restaurant occupied the ground floor of the building. It was sumptuously furnished with old-fashioned chairs and tables, crimson velvet curtains, crystal chandeliers and much ornate gilded plaster work. Near the centre, set on a marble terraced pedestal was a huge glass tank containing live fish, mostly carp, from which the customers could select the one they wanted to eat. I came to the conclusion that the Metropole was a relic from by-gone days, preserved in its entirety, to impress visitors who came to Moscow.

On the occasion of our first visit we were greeted by the Maître d'Hôtel himself, a tall stately gentleman in his early fifties. He was clean-shaven with a pallid complexion but had rather warm-looking, deep brown eyes. His features were heavy and his thinning hair was tinged with grey. He ushered us to a small table at the side which gave us a good view of the restaurant. After he had taken our order and passed it on to one of the waiters he disappeared. Some distance away on the opposite side of the restaurant I had noticed a small table backed by red velvet curtains and half screened by fronds of palms. There was no one sitting there when we came in, but shortly after our drinks arrived it was occupied unobtrusively by two men who just sat there drinking from a carafe of Vodka and smoking innumerable cigarettes. We were watched. The same thing happened on all our subsequent visits, the same tables, the same people. It was an experience, no matter how many times it occurred, which always aroused a feeling of expectancy. In knowing you were being watched, you waited for something to happen. I got to know the name of the Maître d'Hôtel, it was Gabaridze. He was a Georgian who spoke several languages and his English was very good. I complimented him upon it, remarking that he must have been in England to speak it so well. He told me that many years before, he had lived in London and worked in the kitchens of the Savoy Hotel.

When I remarked slyly that he must find his present work very boring, he smiled. We understood one another well! Apart from the few foreign diplomats and business men the place was always filled with Russians. These were men from the far off regions of Russia, factory executives, and commissars, to whom the visit was part of their perks. They ate the plentiful supply of food with gusto and seemed really to enjoy themselves. There were, I noticed, very few women present.

One day about the middle of March I received an unexpected chit from Sir Stafford Cripps requesting me to report to his office the following morning at ten a.m. It was with some misgiving I presented myself the next day, the thought uppermost in my mind being that I was due for a reprimand for associating with a Russian. But it was quite otherwise. After telling me to be seated, Sir Stafford handed me a typescript. 'I thought you might like to read it, Murray. It's Vyshinsky's reply to our protest.'

The gist of the document I read was that the allegations made were totally untrue and unjustified, and were without foundation. The Soviet Government dismissed the charges as absolute fabrication! There was one short paragraph at the end which I well remember, it ran, 'Mr Murray might have been approached, without our knowledge by members of our tobacco industry with an offer of employment as a tobacco specialist, for which he would have in any case been most unsuitable.' Signed A. Vyshinsky. Minister for Internal Affairs.

It was so ridiculous that I could only shrug my shoulders as I handed

92

it back to him.

'There's nothing to worry about, Murray,' he said, 'but I would strongly advise you to write to your parents now and tell them to apply for an exit visa to leave Latvia and Russia!'

It was sound advice and after leaving him, I wrote to my parents at once.

Within a week I received a telegram from my parents saying they had received their exit visa to leave and were already on their way to Moscow. I was overjoyed at the news.

When Nora came that morning to give me my usual Russian lesson, I told her that my parents were arriving from Riga and I would not be taking any more lessons for the next two weeks. She was a bit downcast at this, but brightened up when I told her I'd be definitely continuing them later. I added she could report this to her superiors as it would show she still had my confidence.

I felt really happy and tremendously relieved when the next day I was once more re-united with my parents. They stayed for two weeks. Though I tried to get permission for them to remain in Moscow it was categorically refused. They were precious days. Only the thought that they had to leave and we would be parted once again cast a shadow of sadness over everything. I tried to make them as happy as possible. Rebecca could not do enough for my mother to make her comfortable and my mother in turn stripped her wardrobe of clothes, which she made Rebecca take. Poor Rebecca, she had so very little and my parents had been deeply touched when I recounted her history to them.

One of the places I took them to was the Bolshoi Theatre to see the ballet, *Eugene Onegin*. The ballet was always a great favourite of mine. It was the only time I experienced complete relaxation. I would sit through a performance with half-closed eyes, drinking in the music, hypnotised by the floating dancers before me – a veritable wonderland of sweet music and muted beauty. I saw the now aged Ulanova and also the famous Galina; they danced superbly. The Russians really appreciated their artists, and rightly so. In contrast, Russian films were really pathetic in their childishness. One I saw was about a saboteur who damaged the factory plant and put the blame on the heroine's lover. The heroine had then unmasked the saboteurs, the hero was reinstated and he, not content with getting production back to normal, had actually increased production. The workers then all cheered him and the scene ended with the lovers giving each other an embrace and kiss of such unbelievable chastity, that an American producer would have wept on the spot!

Another I saw was of a poor young peasant who could neither read nor write, when along came a buxom down-to-earth young teacher who soon put him to rights, whereby he was able to become such a capable engineer that all production norms rose to incredible heights – the final scene being the same as the previous film. I did not bother to see any more films, and did not take my parents to see any either. It would have spoilt their wonder and appreciation of the ballet they had seen.

The time however was passing very quickly and my parents seemed happy enough, but there was one piece of news I kept from them, though it was hard to contain my grief. I had received a letter from my cousins in London saying that following a recent air-raid my brother, Nicholas, was missing and presumed dead, as all efforts to trace him had been of no avail. It was a shock to me, but I could only grieve in silence, my main concern being to see that my parents remained troublefree.

The time for them to leave came too soon. It was sad. The only consolation was that we were all well and in good health and so far things had run smoothly. I saw them off and they promised to cable me from Istanbul as soon as they arrived. Three days later I received a telegram to say they had arrived safely and a letter would follow. The letter arrived shortly afterwards and I felt that a great weight had been lifted from my mind. I also felt the emptiness of being once again alone.

It was on a Friday when their letter came and that evening as I sat alone reviewing the events of the past few weeks, the telephone rang. I picked up the receiver.

'John, it's me, Nora. Can I see you please, it's most important.'

'All right, come over but I can't see you for very long,' I said.

I was a bit annoyed. I'd wanted an early night, but I knew that it must be something important Nora wanted to tell me about, because I'd impressed upon her the danger of calling me up on the phone too often.

Within a short while there was a knock on the door. It was

Nora. I led her into the house.

'Well, what's it all about?' I asked.

She sat perched uncomfortably upon the edge of her chair and looked up at me apprehensively.

'It's Major Kirilov,' she began somewhat hesitantly.

'Go on, what about Major Kirilov, what's he done now?' I began jokingly.

But her face was quite serious.

'He's ordered me to bring you to the Hotel Metropole tomorrow night for dinner, and when you are there I am to introduce you to two of his friends who will be waiting for us.' She blurted it out all at once as though glad to get it over with.

'So, we'll tell your Major Kirilov that I'm not coming to any dinner party and what's more I don't want to see him or any of his friends either!' I spoke very emphatically. There was a pause.

Then Nora, still looking at me apprehensively, said in a pleading tone, 'Perhaps, John, you could just see them, just for once, don't you think——' I cut her off.

'No! Nora, I'm sorry but it can't be done. Don't worry, we'll find some other way of pacifying your Major.'

She gave a faint smile, said, 'Oh well,' and left.

Sunday evening came and I was again interrupted by the telephone ringing. It was as I expected, Nora. This time I did not wait, as I was alone in the house, I invited her round.

I could not but help noticing that she looked pale and tired when she came. She looked listless and after greeting me, added in a flat voice, 'I'm going to Leningrad.'

'Going to Leningrad? Why? When?' I asked, quite astonished at this sudden news.

'Tonight, the train leaves in two hours. I'm going to see my Uncle Konstantin.'

'Then don't stay too long, there's my Russian lessons, I'll miss them,' I countered, but there was no answering smile. She did not remain long and seemed very uneasy, but before she left I pressed her to take a little extra money for the lessons I'd had and as an afterthought, took off the little silver wrist-watch I was wearing and gave it to her, knowing that she had always admired it. I felt amply rewarded when I saw how her face lit up at this unexpected gift.

When she had gone, I thought a lot about this young girl who had so innocently become embroiled in espionage, it was a sad thing to my mind.

Some three weeks elapsed, and I did not hear from Nora. Her visit was only to be a short one she had said. I had a presentiment that something had gone wrong somewhere and had begun to feel worried as I felt responsible for her. Further, I realised that I was missing her. Imagine my surprise one day when I was given a note that had been left at the gate for me.

It was from Nora. Vasily, the porter who gave me the letter, explained that a poorly-dressed little old woman had handed it to him saying that it was to be given to no one but 'Mister John'. Although he was supposed to let his superior know of anything unusual happening, he assured me that he had not reported it. Funnily enough, I believed him, and I think he did speak the truth.

The note from Nora was short. It was written in German and gave me her address. She simply said she was staying there, but was very ill and was so sorry to trouble me, but the people with whom she was staying had very little of anything themselves in the way of food and she would have to leave soon.

It was a pathetic little note and I read between the lines. Now the staff of the Moscow Embassy, in view of its unique situation and the food shortages in Russia, had an arrangement whereby wines and spirits and canned beers and provisions could be purchased in bulk, duty free, from England, and transported to Moscow under a special diplomatic dispensation once a year. These supplies were not only for personal use, but also to enable the staff to undertake their obligations as regards social get-togethers with other Embassy and Consular staff. This was a form of liaison quite important for Foreign Office personnel living abroad. By a lucky chance, the last orders that were to be permitted for many years were just being made up when I arrived in Moscow, so with Bagshawe I was able to stock up with a considerable amount of provisions. From our stores I made up a parcel of tinned provisions, soups, meats, cereals. I also enclosed an envelope with several hundred roubles and a note saying 'Get well quick, John.' I got hold of Valentina, gave her the address and asked her to deliver the parcel

Above: The author with his parents, baby sister and younger brother Nicholas (left of picture).
Below: A photo taken on Armistice Day 1936 of the choir to the British Church in Riga, Latvia. From l. to r. standing: the author, his cousin Flora, his brother Nicholas, Mr John Watson (reputed British Agent), Mr Cox (Union Cold Storage Manager) and Helen Bisseniek. Seated in middle row on extreme right: Mrs Bisseniek whose husband was liquidated during the Soviet annexation of Latvia. Bottom row from l. to r.: Miss Bisseniek, the younger of Mrs Bisseniek's daughters and third from the left, Anne, cousin of the author.

Above: King George V's Requiem Mass held in the British Church at Riga, conducted by th[e] Rev. Harrison. *Below:* The author at the start of his long vigil in Latvia.

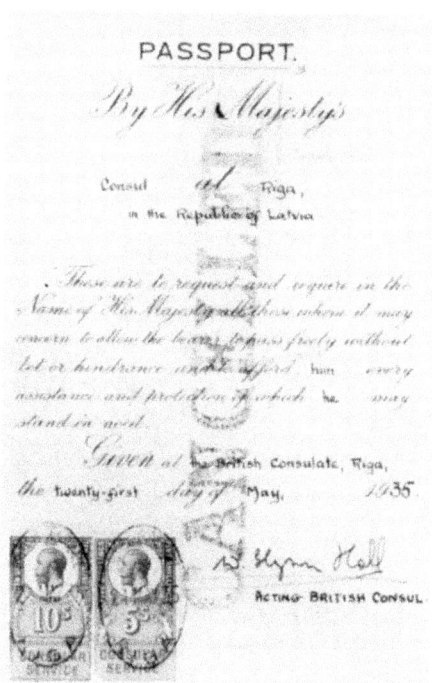

PASSPORT.

By His Majesty's

Consul *at* Riga,
in the Republic of Latvia

*These are to request and require in the
Name of His Majesty all those whom it may
concern to allow the bearer to pass freely without
let or hindrance and to afford him every
assistance and protection of which he may
stand in need.*

*Given at the British Consulate, Riga,
the twenty-first day of May, 1935.*

W. Glynn Hall

ACTING BRITISH CONSUL.

Above: The author in Riga, October 1940, before leaving for Moscow. *Below:* The cover from the author's passport showing the signature of W. Glynn Hall, Acting British Consul, in Riga.

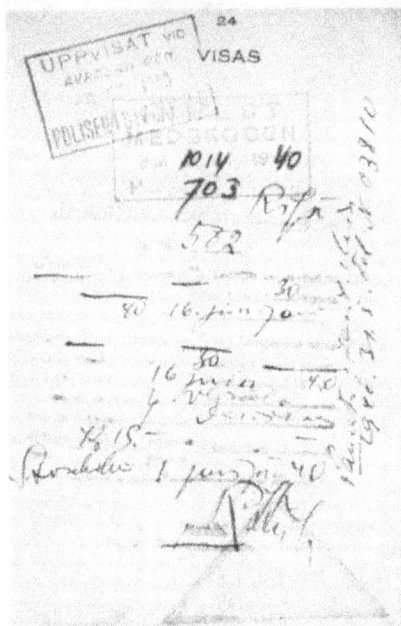

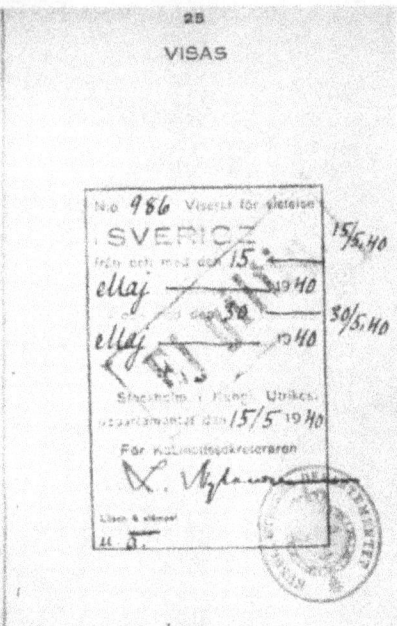

Above: Page 24 from the author's passport showing the entry visa into Sweden from Norway after his escape during the German invasion. *Below:* The author's Diplomatic Identity Card whilst working at the British Embassy, Moscow.

April 28

Dear Mr. Murray,

I have just opened the box in the hall and found your note and your most welcome contribution to the Prisoners of War Parcels fund. We are very grateful for it, and it is good of you to promise us a contribution every month. Thank you very much indeed.

Yours sincerely

Theresa Cripps

A letter from Lady Theresa Cripps, wife of the British Ambassador, to the author, on 28 April, 1941.

Nora – The Swallow.

BRITISH EMBASSY,
MOSCOW.
KUIBYSHEV:

October 23rd. 1941.

The Principal, Sea Transport Office:

Port of Disembarkation.

Mr. J. Murray is being transferred to Home Establishment from the British Embassy, Moscow, for reasons of health.

It is requested that he be furnished with a warrant and an advance of sterling for travelling expenses to enable him to report to the Director of Allied and Foreign Liaison, Princes House, Air Ministry.

Air Vice-Marshal,
Head of British Air Mission,
in te U.S.S.R.

Above: The Hotel Metropole, Moscow. The first floor suite housed the Soviet Espionage Headquarters. *Below:* The order transferring the author to Home Establishment 'For reasons of health' following the discovery of his liaison with Nora.

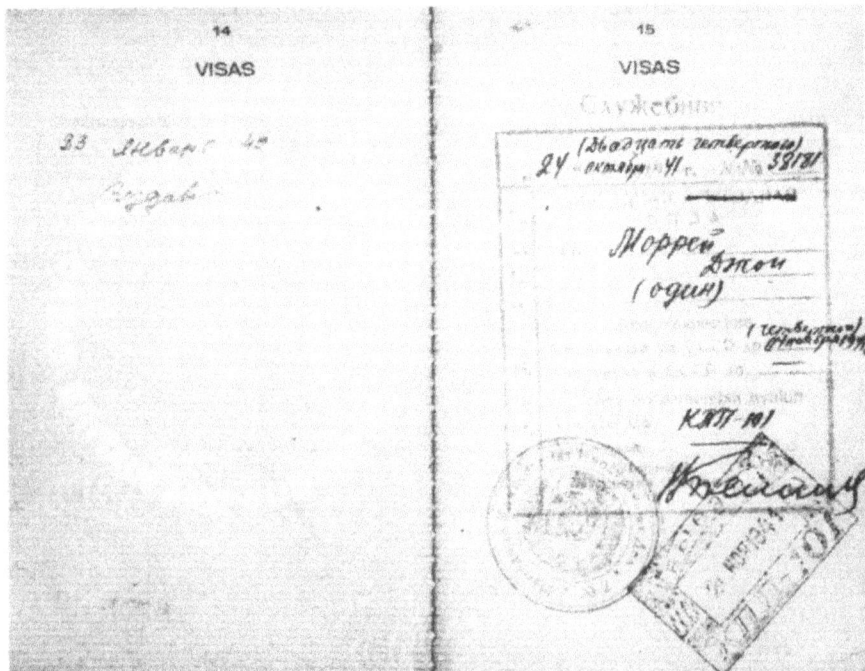

Above: The order recalling the author from aboard the S.S. *Temple Arch. Below:* Page 14 of the author's passport showing the stamp of the official Soviet Marriage Bureau, denoting his marriage in the Soviet Union.

Место
для штампа

Гр. _Маррей_
        фамилия,
    Джон
    имя,   отчество

Гр-ка _Корниенко_
              фамилия,
    Нина - Нора _Васильевна_
        имя,   отчество

ступили в брак, о чём в книге записей актов гражданского состояния о браке за

_двадцать третьяго Января тысяча девять-
сот сорок второго года 23/I-42._
прописью и цифрами год, число и месяц

роизведена соответствующая запись под № _57_

амилия после заклю-   он _Маррей Д._
чения брака   она _Маррей Н-Н В_

5 марта _1942_ г.

Зав. Бюро ЗАГС

Делопроизводитель

Above: Nora and the author on their Wedding Day in Archangel, 23 January, 1942. *Below:*
The Soviet Marriage Certificate given to Nora on 5 March, 1942 which enabled her to
acquire a British Passport.

Joseph Stalin *Radio Times Hulton Picture Library*

Sir Stafford Cripps *Radio Times Hulton Picture Library*

Lieut. General Sir Noel Mason-MacFarlane *Keystone*

To: Mr. J. Murray, Archangel.

From: Group Captain I.C. Bird,
          Senior Royal Air Force Officer, Archangel.
Date: 5/2/42.

Ref: ICB/22.

            Notice of termination of employment.

        You are hereby notified that your appointment
as clerk to the Air Attaché, Moscow, will terminate
one month from today's date.

                                    J.C.Bird,
                            Group Captain,
                        S.R.A.F.O., Archangel.

Above: Notice of the author's termination of employment after his marriage because of security reasons. *Below:* S.S. *Empire Stevenson.* Photograph by *courtesy Messrs. Wm. Brown Atkinson & Co. Ltd., Hull*

OFFICIAL LOG of the *S/S Empire Stevenson*

from *At Archangel* towards

Date and Hour of the Occurrence	Place of the Occurrence, or situation by Latitude and Longitude at Sea.	Date of Entry.	Entries required by Act of Parliament.	Master of Proof of Reference indeed.

19.1.42   Archangel   19.1.42   This day Robert Radford (Greaser) and James Wadham (Fireman) were discharged from hospital and are now able to carry on with their normal duties.

H. Terrell master

J. Ernest Mate.

24.4.42   Mololovsk   27/4/42   Mr John Murray and Mrs Nina Nora Murray were signed on articles as asst Stuard and Stewardess respectively

H. Terrell master

W. x Junior mate.

1.20 PM

15.5.42   Mololovsk   15/5/42   Whilst having gun drill on 12 pounder A.A. Norman Anderson (OS) who was loading the gun failed to get his right hand away before breach was closed by Alexander Duguid (AB). N. Anderson had the tips of his third finger taken off on right hand. He was taken to hospital and attended but not detained.

H. Terrell master

Doctor says he can resume work in 3 days.

A page from the Log Book of S.S. *Empire Stevenson* where Nora and the author were signed on as Stewardess and Asst. Steward respectively to cover their identities.

EMPIRE STAR
Frederick Leyland & Co.; 1935; Harland & Wolff; 12,656 tons; 524·2×70·4×32·3; 12,000 b.h.p.; 16 knots; oil engines.
The *Empire Star*, Capt. S. N. Capon, was torpedoed and sunk by a German submarine in the North Atlantic on October 23rd, 1942. Four men were killed on board. The captain's boat with 26 crew, six gunners and six passengers was never seen again.

EMPIRE STATESMAN
Ministry of Shipping (Runciman Shipping Co.); 1920; G. Ansaldo & Co.; 5,306 tons; 379×51·5×28·3; 606 n.h.p.; oil engines.
The British cargo ship *Empire Statesman* sailed from Freetown on November 19th, 1940, on a voyage to Oban and Middlesbrough with an ore cargo. She reported engine trouble two days later but no subsequent news of the ship was received. She carried a crew of 32.

EMPIRE STEEL
Ministry of War Transport (Andrew Weir & Co.); 1941; Cammell Laird & Co.; 8,138 tons; 465·3×59·3×33·8; 502 n.h.p.; 10 knots; oil engines.
The motorship *Empire Steel* was torpedoed and sunk by a German submarine on March 24th, 1942, in the North Atlantic. She carried a crew of 47 of whom 39 were killed.

EMPIRE STEVENSON
Ministry of War Transport (W. Brown, Atkinson & Co.); 1941; J. Readhead & Sons; 6,029 tons; 405·8×53·5×33·3; 415 n.h.p.; triple-expansion engines.
The steamship *Empire Stevenson*, on a voyage from Hull to North Russia, was torpedoed by a German aircraft, blew up and sank on September 13th, 1942, off the North Cape. All on board were lost, 40 crew and 19 gunners.

EMPIRE STREAM
Ministry of War Transport (J. S. Stranaghan & Co.); 1941; Lithgows; 2,922 tons; 315·2×44·4×19·9; 240 n.h.p.; triple-expansion engines.
The steamship *Empire Stream*, on a voyage from Gibraltar to Dundee, was torpedoed and sunk by a German submarine on September 25th, 1941, about 800 miles W. of Cape Finisterre. Four of her crew, two gunners and two stowaways were killed.

Above: The Obituary of S.S. *Empire Stevenson*, sunk with all hands on her return journey to Russia, 13 September, 1942. *Dictionary of Disasters at Sea by Charles Hocking. Below:* Troop Movement Order transferring Nora and the author to an American troopship for the final leg of journey home from Iceland, 12 July, 1942.

The author (left) with his brother Nicholas in England, October, 1943. They had last met in Riga, Latvia in 1938. They both thought each other had been killed until by accident they met on Northallerton Station during an air raid alarm. The author had enlisted in the Intelligence Corps, 1943. Nicholas was in the RASC.

to Nora, who I'd heard was ill. I blurted out that if she wished she could also report the matter to the NKVD – the matter meant nothing to me, as Nora was only my teacher and I would do as much for anyone who was ill and in trouble. Do you know, women are women the world over? She gave me a kind of mysterious smile and looked straight at me.

'Don't worry, Mr Murray, it will be all right.'

I left it at that. Valentina delivered the parcel and returned in a very serious mood. 'Your Nora is very ill. She has inflammation of the lungs. She cried when I gave her your parcel, but she is very, very grateful to you.'

I thanked her. She still gave me that pitying half-smile.

One day soon after this incident my chief called me into his office and told me that instructions had been received from the Foreign Office that the Embassy was to reduce its staff to essential personnel only and all the redundant staff together with the womenfolk were to be sent back to England. Amongst those to go were all those living at *Maly kharitonevsky* except myself. Sir Stafford had decided that I should move into one of the vacant furnished cottages that were situated in the rear garden of the Embassy grounds itself. This suited me, but I asked about the staff we employed. The outcome was that both Rebecca and Vasily the porter should remain as caretakers, and Shura the chauffeur should be paid off as I had no car and in any case would not require one. With regards to Valentina the cook, she could still be employed as such at my new place, should she so desire.

When I saw Bagshawe later that day his first words were, 'You've heard the news, John?' I nodded. 'Do you know,' he continued, 'I'm glad I'm going. It'll be good to get back home again!'

I told him about the plans that had been made for me regarding my new home.

'You'll be better off there. This is an unlucky place,' he said.

'Never mind,' I said. 'I'll get the lads together and we'll give you one hell of a party at my place, so you'll have a real good send off.' At the idea of the party to be held in my new home Bagshawe began right away to prepare the invitations.

We called Valentina in and told her about the new state of affairs and I asked her if she would like to continue at my new place. She was not only delighted, but grateful. It was arranged that I should still eat at *Maly kharitonevsky* for the next couple of days until Bagshawe left. I told her that her first job with me would be to prepare for the best party she'd ever organised, for Mr Bagshawe who was leaving.

It was a Friday and Bagshawe was going on the following Monday so our party was scheduled for Sunday evening. As I was leaving the house after lunch, Vasily handed me a note. It was from Nora. It simply said, 'Tomorrow at noon in the park.' Throughout the time since receiving the first note some three weeks ago, I had sent several parcels of food, with money, to Nora through Valentina who had told me she was gradually getting better. I never expected a written reply as it was quite possible that Nora could not trust Valentina. Receiving this note now, I knew something had happened to Nora. Luckily Saturday was my day off.

Making use of the large crowds to shake off any followers I dodged in and out and slipped into the *Krasny dvor* underground station and boarded a train to Sokolniki Park.

It was not long before I saw Nora, she looked awful and I was shocked to see how pale and thin she was.

'Hello, Nora, having trouble?' I tried to speak lightly.

She said nothing, opening her handbag she took out her passport and handed it to me.

I examined it wonderingly. Underneath her photo, across the place of residence, a thick black line had been drawn. To a Russian, this meant that the owner was no longer entitled to reside in Moscow, and further, should the owner be picked up by the Militia he or she would be liable to instant arrest followed by deportation from Moscow to a place of exile.

I handed it back, all I could think of was to ask how this all came about. I could see she was still pretty weak, so we found a deserted bench and sat down.

She told me her story in a listless, faraway voice as though nothing really mattered any more.

Before she had come to see me on the night she left for Leningrad, she already knew all was lost. She'd had to report to Major Kirilov my adamant refusal to meet himself and his colleagues. His reaction had been one of violent rage. He had stormed and raved at her that she was a traitor and an agent of the capitalist dogs. That she was no longer to be trusted and had let the wicked and dangerous Englishman she was supposed to have watched make fools of them all. At this point she had protested saying that I was not the wicked man he thought I was, and that on the contrary I was a kindly person who had a great affection for the Russian people. This only increased his outburst of rage, and he had turned on her and accused her of falling in love with me instead of doing her duty. He said that it was no good her protesting, they had been watching her all the time. With that he ordered her to give him her passport, cancelled it, and then flung it back at her saying, 'See if your damned Englishman can help you now!' He then shouted at her to get out and leave Moscow immediately, warning her that if she did not do so, or attempted to see me again, she would be arrested and pay the full penalty as a traitor to her country.

In spite of the threat she decided she would see me before she left for Leningrad.

'Why didn't you tell me all this before?' I asked her, remembering how strange she had acted the last time I saw her.

'Because I knew how worried you were about your parents coming and I did not want to add further to your troubles,' she replied.

She then went on to tell me how after arriving in Leningrad she had gone to her uncle's flat, but for his own and her aunt's safety, he had refused to let her stay more than a couple of days. She then contacted a former friend of her father's, a woman whom she knew as Nina. Nina had pretended to be very kind to her, they had exchanged confidences and she had told Nina about her troubles and friendship with me.

Within a matter of twenty-four hours she was picked up by the Leningrad secret police for interrogation. Her so-called friend Nina had proved to be an informer!

She was kept in the cells all that night under constant observation and questioning. In a last desperate effort to clear herself she revealed to them that actually she was a Soviet agent working for the special branch of security under the *nom-de-plume* of 'The Swallow'. They asked her why she had not mentioned this before, and she told them she could not for security reasons. Shortly afterwards she was released and told she must leave Leningrad and return to Moscow. When she arrived in Moscow, she had nowhere to go and, frightened of being picked up again before deciding how she could contact me, had taken refuge in a cemetery. That night, the cold and dampness of the graveyard had made her very ill. Delirious, she had been found by a kindly old woman whose custom was to search the deserted cemetery at dusk for anything that could be used for fuel. She had managed to get her home and nurse her. It was this brave old lady who had brought me the first note and the second. The illness had developed into pneumonia, but the old lady had continued to nurse and look after her even though she had very little herself. The food and money I had sent saved her life and for this she was very grateful. Two days ago however the old lady informed her that the house porter had reported her to the police who were now enquiring about the unregistered guest she was sheltering.

She realised then that the net was tightening around her and how hopeless her situation was, that it would only be a matter of hours before she would again be arrested. Her one thought was to see me once more, if only to thank me for the kindness I had shown her.

It would be hard to describe the thoughts and feelings I experienced as I listened to this hurried narrative. She had sat all the while with her hands clasped upon her lap. I put my hands over hers, they were ice-cold. Leaning forward I said, very softly, 'Nora, tell me, is it true what Major Kirilov said? Do you really love me?' She hung her head and was silent. Only as the hot tears began to fall upon the back of my hands clasped around hers did I realise she was crying.

For me, that was enough! I stood up. In my agitation I paced up and down trying to gather my thoughts as to what course of action I should take. The biggest shock was the fact that this girl was actually in love with me. It seemed so unbelievable and was something I'd not even dreamed of as possible. The whole situation was so absurd, there was nobody I could turn to for advice. I knew I'd be out on my neck if anybody in the Embassy knew of my predicament for, already whilst listening to her story, the full horrors of her plight had become evident to me and I knew it was partly my fault. Another thing, although our relationship had been 'strictly business' as far as I was concerned, I suddenly realised how I had missed her and the strange empty feeling I experienced whilst she had been away.

Without giving the matter any further thought, I made an instant decision. I told her about my new accommodation arrangements and explained to her how one could reach the cottage where I now lived. It meant passing the guards at the main gates to the Embassy. She was to say Mr Murray had sent her if questioned and ask for Mr Velukin. With that, I drew from my pocket the spare key to the cottage, took both her hands in mine and pressed the key into them.

'Nora,' I said, 'this is the key to my house. Go there and wait until I come home.'

I did not wait for her reply, but turned quickly on my heels and strode away without looking back. The matter was now out of my hands, if she was there when I returned, I knew that it would be Fate that had decreed it so. There was nothing more I could do, to have accompanied her myself would have been fatal once my shadows picked me up again.

I made my way to Bagshawe's place first, as I had still to arrange quite a number of things, which included extra staff for my party the next evening. Two hours later, Shura was driving me back to the Embassy. When I entered my cottage it was dark and silent. I went to the sitting room and switched on the light. From an arm-chair in the far corner, a puffed, tear-stained face looked up at me – it was Nora. She sprang to her feet and put her arms around me, 'John, Oh John,' she murmured as I held her tight. She was warm and soft and clinging. I tasted the salt of her tear-stained face. We made love that night. Nora was the first woman to whom I had ever made love. She was twenty-one – I was thirty-three. All through the years up to that moment I had imagined what love would be like, from the guilty stage of early adolescence to my older, more reflective years. But I had had very little to do with girls and I was never popular with them, being of a far too serious disposition and somewhat old-fashioned in my ways.

That night was one I shall never forget. Nora gave me every-thing that a woman could give a man and I was intoxicated by the release and power of the passions which had remained pent-up for all those years. It was not only the physical ecstasy of being one with her, it was the aftermath that was so wonderful – that feeling of unutterable sweetness and tenderness that permeated our whole beings. As I looked upon her lying at my side, I sensed the indescribable happiness that enveloped us both and vowed within myself that should anyone dare to lay hands on Nora, I'd tear them apart with my bare hands, for she was now of me as I was of her, with our very lifestreams already mingling and coursing through each other's veins.

Just before we finally fell asleep, troubled as I was by conflicting thoughts on the dangerous consequences of bringing Nora inside the Embassy grounds, it occurred to me to ask her why she had sought refuge in the cemetery. It was a trivial matter, but I had to know everything now my mind was made up. She then told me the story, a story so incredible that it could only happen in a place like Russia. It would take far too long to give the full narrative, but the gist of her story was as follows.

As she had hurried down a small dark side street after leaving the station on her return from Leningrad, she heard footsteps behind her. Glancing round she saw an NKVD officer. He called on her to stop, and grasped her arm. She tried to struggle free.

'Don't be afraid Nora Vasilievna,' he said. 'I am a friend, I knew your father, Vasily Savich. Come with me, I must talk to you.'

The tone of his voice reassured her and they walked some distance together in silence, she wondering all the time about the meaning of this strange encounter. He led her into a 'traktir', the Russian equivalent to our pubs, where one could get a drink – they soon had a small table to themselves, the other customers melted away on seeing the NKVD officer.

Her companion ordered a carafe of Vodka and though she drank very little, he drank continually, filling the small glass and emptying it in great gulps. In between he spoke.

'Norachka, you don't know me do you?'

She shook her head.

'That is well, it is better so,' he said and continued, 'your father Vasily Savich and I were great friends, when you were a baby I often dangled you upon my knee. Your father was a good man and a brave one, a true patriot. When he was arrested I was shocked, I knew he was innocent, but that is how it goes in Russia today.'

He paused to fill himself another glass of Vodka and continued. 'Listen carefully Norachka, you are in great danger. An order has been issued that you are to be arrested as soon as you are found and executed immediately, it is my department that deals with such orders. Believe me Norachka, I have to deal with many such. Up until now I have been able to protect you by keeping this order back, but I can do so no longer!'

She had listened not knowing what to say and he continued, 'It was me who handled the enquiry from Leningrad and I've been waiting around for your return. It is only God's will that I have seen you today. There is so little time left, yes, so very, very little time left.' He looked at his watch.

'Norachka, tonight I leave for the front, my train goes in one hour's time.'

'What front?' she had asked. 'There is no war.'

'Ah, Norachka, you do not know of what is happening. Shortly, maybe in a month's time we shall be at war with the German dogs who seek to invade our Russia, but we will destroy them, have no fear, but there will be hard times, such hard times as none can imagine.

'Yes, very hard times, and I . . .' he shook his head from side to side. 'I will not return alive, I feel it in my bones. God knows what will happen to my daughter.

'Yes Norachka, I have a daughter, a young and beautiful girl just like you. Perhaps God will be good and provide a protector for her too when I am gone; who knows? Now, Norachka, I can do no more for you. You must go. Go far away from Moscow and keep away from the big towns, anywhere, but you must go.'

He stood up and thrust a handful of notes into her hand. 'Here, take this my child, and God bless you and guard you! Above all, do not confide in anyone ever again, there are informers everywhere!'

With that he saw her to the door and returned to his table where she noticed the empty carafe of Vodka had been replaced with a full one.

She had then wandered through the streets avoiding the

crowded places, gradually working her way from the centre of the city to its outskirts. She felt tired and confused. There was no place she could go to and her fear of being arrested gradually increased to terror. Above all, she wanted to be alone, to think quietly what to do next. Although it was cold she felt hot and giddy and her limbs began to feel dead. She came to a churchyard, the gates long since gone and the stillness seemed so inviting to her now weakening body. She went through the portals and staggered among the graves and finally knew no more until she opened her eyes and found herself lying in a strange bed with the anxious-faced old lady bending over her.

As she finished her story she shivered and began to tremble.

'There, there, Nora, it's all right, don't be frightened, no one will touch you now!' I said, and held her tightly in my arm meanwhile caressing her face with my free hand.

She murmured something, and fell asleep. I was satisfied. Now, I knew what to do! I had done the right thing in bringing her to my home.

There was no doubt in my mind that it was going to be a very tough job protecting her. But Nora's narrative, coupled with what I had learned from her about Major Kirilov, led me to the conclusion that his department, being a very special one, shunned publicity and acted with such secrecy that not even the ordinary police were taken into their confidence. She would have certainly been arrested long ago if this had not been the case, and it was this that gave me hope. From now on her future was my responsibility.

In the early hours of that late May morning of 1941 I awoke and with the approaching cold grey dawn, the full realisation of our predicament became depressingly apparent.

Nora lay beside me, quietly breathing and fast asleep. I looked upon her face, so beautiful and sweet in its relaxation. My determination hardened; somehow, some way, I would marry her and get her out of Russia to safety. Nothing else mattered. I began cold-bloodedly to review the situation. The NKVD had now no further use for Nora – she was a discredited agent. Furthermore, she had betrayed their trust and vengeance would be swift and merciless if they could lay hands on her. For the time being, whilst in the Embassy grounds, she was safe, and they could not touch her. For me to appeal to the Embassy would be hopeless. I had brought her to my house without approval or permission. I would be shipped off home immediately and then, God knows what would happen to Nora. It did not bear thinking of. I'd got Bagshawe's party on that day. How could I explain Nora's presence?

The only staff I had was Valentina. She was commencing her duties with me as from that day but her hours of work were from nine a.m. until three p.m., after which she would return home, so for the party at least, a waitress would be needed to serve the food and drinks, and to tidy up – this would provide a legitimate excuse for having Nora – she would be the waitress! No one else knew of her existence except Bagshawe and Valentina. Valentina, I knew would be surprised to see Nora. I also knew she would have to report Nora's presence at my place, but that could not be helped. All I and Nora could do, would be to wait and see what transpired, and hope for the best. When Nora awoke, I explained my idea to her.

Her first reaction was, 'But I've no clothes! Only the black dress I've been wearing!'

'Don't worry,' I said. 'You look beautiful as you are, but I'll go over to see Rebecca at *Maly kharitonevsky* and get you a nice little pinafore to wear,' and as I gave her a kiss, added, 'And you'll be the world's most wonderful waitress!'

Valentina arrived and got the shock of her life when she saw Nora, but I explained in quite a matter-of-fact manner that I'd brought her in to help at the party. I went to Bagshawe's place and told him his party was going to be a real good one, and also mentioned that I had managed to find Nora who was going to give me a hand with the serving. He thought it was a fine idea. I saw Rebecca, who willingly lent me one of her aprons, I then returned home.

The evening was a huge success. Most of the junior members came from our Embassy staff. Bagshawe's chief, Captain Clanchy did not come, neither did my chief, but Colonel Greer representing the Services, and his secretary Jimes came. Quite a number of our friends from the American Embassy arrived, including Reinhardt. From the other Consulates, the

Greeks, Turks and Persians came, and of course the newspaper men who could never be kept out of anything. Besides these there was a fair contingent of staff from our late Legations in Czechoslovakia, Hungary and Yugoslavia who had been unable to get home when the Germans invaded those countries and had found temporary asylum in Moscow.

For the party I had laid on plenty of drinks, several wines, whisky, gin and Vodka. The food Valentina had prepared consisted of hundreds of open sandwiches, Swedish Smörgåsbord fashion, of every variety of meats, cheeses and fish, all beautifully garnished. Fresh fruit, of course, was not available, but we had a large variety of tinned fruits. The *pièce de résistance* at the end of the evening was, of course, ice-cream served with champagne, which was a Russian fashion. Valentina was proud of her ice-cream which she made from quarts of fresh cream in a hand-operated freezer, which used to be lent out and around the Embassy for party-givers on such occasions. All enjoyed themselves, and a real friendly atmosphere pervaded. I was both congratulated and chipped about the new waitress I'd found. Jimes, who though married, always had an eye for a pretty face and legs, was most attentive to Nora, who carried out her duties as quietly and efficiently as a real waitress. The party finally came to an end at about two a.m. Normally it would have gone on much longer, but as many of the guests were leaving Moscow in only about another eight hours, it helped to bring the party to a close. All I wanted, was to be alone with Nora. I was so frightened that our hours of happiness might be short.

But it had been a good party and I was so pleased that I'd been able to give Bagshawe a good send-off as I'd promised. In a way I was sorry to see him go because I knew that at heart he was one of the best.

The days that followed were ones of bliss. But I had to work hard and late; things were happening. The messages we decoded from London were full of portent and they made me think. Of course, we did not discuss them even among ourselves. You just carried on doing your job regardless. Nora was happy and content to stay in the house. We would walk round the garden during the now warm nights. I'd warned her never to leave the Embassy garden, and this she understood.

I could not help feeling a little apprehensive sometimes, and it was Velukin, the Russian messenger, who gave me the first hint of what was happening. I often had brief chats with Velukin who told me he was married with a wife and two children. He told me he hated the job he was doing and felt very insecure. I understood. His masters, the NKVD were an unpredictable lot. He also sensed I understood his position. I always gave him a cheery greeting when I encountered him of a morning, and occasionally would give him a knowing wink, which made him smile. Three days after Bagshawe's departure, he approached me and said in a low tone, 'Mr Murray, you have a citizeness, Korzhenko, staying in your house. It's not good. Send her away or THEY will make a lot of trouble for you.'

'No! I like Russia, but I love my Russian girl and I am going to marry her and make her my wife, and you can tell that to THEM,' I said heatedly. He just shrugged his shoulders.

'It's so difficult – I only wanted to warn you.'

So, this is the first round of the battle I'm going to have on my hands, I thought.

Nora seemed very downcast that evening, and she told me she didn't know why. 'But you shouldn't be sad,' I said, 'I'm going to marry you and take you back to England.' It was the first time I had mentioned my intentions. She looked at me and laughed.

'But that's impossible, you know it is.'

'No, nothing is impossible if we truly love one another. Shall I read you the cards?' I added.

'What do you mean?' she asked.

I produced an old pack of playing cards from one of the drawers in the dresser, and whilst shuffling them explained to her that my mother was Irish and like the gypsies, the Irish had strange powers.

Now I'd watched my mother many times when I was a boy tell neighbours their fortunes – they were always women who'd had some trouble or other, or who were beset with fears of some sort. My mother would firmly state she was not a fortune-teller, but could only read and interpret the cards that they blindly selected from the pack. She would lay them face down on the table and they would select a given number from them. Needless to say, my mother was very shrewd besides being wise, and somehow the portents always fitted in with the events that later transpired.

Did I believe in such powers myself? I do not know. I am one of those persons who strongly disclaims any supposition to be superstitious. Nevertheless, I always threw salt over my left shoulder if I spilt any, if you know what I mean.

Nora looked at me wonderingly and I saw the gradual excitement of anticipation light up in her eyes. I began by selecting sixteen cards – the four queens, the four jacks, the four aces and the four deuces. I did not show them to her but simply laid them face downwards on the table and shuffled them around. She watched me intently. 'Now, don't think about anything at all, just pick out four cards and give them to me without looking at them!'

She selected four cards at random and handed them to me. Even I did not know what to expect. Slowly, one by one, I turned the cards over and placed them face upwards on the table in front of me, pushed the remainder to one side and turned them face upwards also.

By an amazing coincidence, she had selected the very cards I was hoping for. They were the Queen of Hearts, the Jack of Spades, the two of Hearts and the Ace of Clubs.

'Look,' I said, 'from all the cards on the table, you have picked the Queen of Hearts. That is your card. You are all heart, throughout your life whatever you do, or wherever you go you will be dominated by the heart. There is nothing but good in the heart and it will protect you from all evil. Had you picked the Queen of Diamonds that would have told me you were hard, unrelenting and avaricious, with no thought but of yourself. The Club would have told me you were of a restless dissatisfied character, for ever bemoaning your lot, and if you had picked the Queen of Spades, that would have meant that you were evil and mean and would bring nothing but harm to all those around you. In fact,' I continued, 'if you had picked up anything other than the Queen of Hearts, I would have run away and left you as quick as I could!'

'But the other cards. What about them?'

I could see she was impressed and longing for me to continue.

'See, here we have the Jack of Spades. This is the man that Fate has chosen for your partner. He is young and dark, he should have been Hearts, but really he is Hearts, and it is only the evils of darkness that surround him and cast the shadows over his card that appear as darkness, but in any case, this young man is bound to you, for the next card is the two of Hearts which means the first two cards you have picked will be joined in love and happiness, two hearts on one card!' I nodded impressively.

'Is it you?' she whispered.

'Why, of course it's me!' I answered. 'It's all here, in the cards you've picked yourself. They don't lie! But see, now we have the last card – it's the Ace of Clubs. The Clubs among other things represent your home or dwelling. It means a new home for you; the white space that surrounds the Club denotes the sea. Surely it is a home far away, beyond the seas and surrounded by the seas. Why, that must be England!'

She looked at me in awed silence. I felt elated.

'Tell me more,' she commanded.

'I've not finished yet,' I said, as I gathered all the cards together and shuffled them. 'Here, you shuffle them now,' I said. After she had finished I took them and counted out four packs of thirteen each, laying them out face downwards.

'In one of these packs, my Queen, your card will appear and all the cards that surround it, will be the ones that will tell me your future!'

I could feel the mounting curiosity and excitement I had aroused, and I began to feel infected with it myself. I examined the first pack for Nora's card, then the second pack, and then the third pack. With a flourish I picked up the fourth pack and began to lay the cards down face upwards in the shape of a cross. Then an incredible thing happened, which even I took for an omen. The Ace of Hearts appeared in the centre of the cross, with the Queen of Hearts appearing to the left and the Jack of Spades to the right of it. Above the Ace of Hearts came the two of Hearts. A mixture of cards formed the rest of the cross.

'There you are!' I cried. 'Look, everything is confirmed. There's you, there's me, there's the Ace of Hearts – the greatest of all Love cards and the two of Hearts above us, which means we two shall be joined together!'

I grabbed Nora and we danced round the table like a couple of excited kids. After dancing around for a couple of minutes, Nora wanted to know what the rest of the cards had to say. I explained that the Ace of Clubs which had turned up, really meant that she would cross water to a new home, especially as it was backed by the two of Clubs which confirmed the presence of two homes divided by a space which meant water. There were Hearts and Diamonds which I said denoted surprises, presents, and all things nice. There were the black cards, especially the Spades, which I said were the cards of ill-omen of the trials, sufferings, sorrows, and tears to come. She looked apprehensive at this, but I told her I had to read all the cards for her, the good with the bad, if I was to be truthful.

She was not to worry because the very centre was subordinated to the Ace of Hearts which finally triumphed over everything, through the love, happiness, and warmth of heart that bound us together. This had all taken time, and by the end of it Nora's sadness had vanished. That night as we lay together, I felt teardrops running down her cheek onto mine. She was fast asleep, dreaming. Whether they were tears of joy or of sadness, I did not know, but I held her gently but firmly more close to me.

The next morning, Nora was bright and sunny again and I felt cheerful as I went into the Embassy for duty, glad indeed that my ploy of the evening before had worked. But a shock awaited me when I started my duties that morning. I was summoned into the presence of Mr John Dunlop, the Embassy Secretary.

There was no beating about the bush: 'I hear you have a Russian woman in your employ as housekeeper, Murray?'

'That's right,' I said.

'But it is not all right. You know that no staff is permitted to be employed here without the sanction of the Burobin,* and I have just received a notification from them about this matter. Will you please see that she leaves immediately!'

I protested that I had to give her time to leave and he said she must go as soon as possible.

---

* Burobin: The state bureau for supplying domestic staff to foreign embassies and consulates.

I did not tell Nora, as I was determined to keep her on. A week passed and I was again summoned to Dunlop.

'The Burobin inform me that your housekeeper is still on the Embassy premises. Really, Murray, you must do something about it!'

I told him that I had not forgotten his instructions, but the difficulty was that she was in trouble with the Soviet authorities and I dare not let her go until I had at least made some preparations for her safety, which just at the moment was difficult owing to the volume of work which had increased so enormously lately. He understood what I meant. We were really quite good friends. The point was, he was in authority. In the end it was agreed I should do what I could, as soon as I could, to resolve the matter. I did not tell Nora about this either. The work was growing – we were already working late in the evenings, busy decoding the stream of messages from the Service Departments that multiplied in number each day. The only heartening thing about them was that they also told of decreasing air activity over England and consequently lower casualties and damage to our armament production. It was already well into June and in the early summer mornings, rising early, Nora and I often peered through the curtains to watch Sir Stafford Cripps taking his morning exercise, striding quickly with his long legs. Nora told me that she thought our Ambassador looked a very stern and severe man indeed. I told her it was not so, that he was actually a very kind and human man, who was what I would consider a real socialist.

To keep Nora occupied I had managed to get some books and plenty of writing materials for her, thus she was able to continue her studies on her own – in between looking, or perhaps I should say, loving me and looking after the cottage, there being no hope of her visiting her University. I still employed Valentina, but she and Nora did not get on together; Nora had her own private room and she always retired to that when Valentina arrived. I had to keep Valentina on because she did the shopping, but my chief reason was I did not want to give the NKVD a handle to start something by dismissing her.

Part V

War comes to the Soviet Union

On the night of 21 June, 1941, Nora and I went to bed earlier than usual as I was exceptionally tired and we soon fell asleep in each other's arms. We seemed no sooner to have fallen asleep when we were awakened by the long drawn-out howl of what seemed to us, a wolf. Then another, and another, and then several creatures took up the howling. It sounded spine-chilling in those early hours of the morning. We got up; I looked at the clock, it was two-thirty a.m. It seemed almost a portent of what was to come. I knew what it was. When I had first come to the cottage, Velukin had asked me how I liked it. I'd told him jokingly, 'fine', now that I had a back wall to nip over when I wanted to dodge my unwelcome shadowers. He had instantly become alarmed.

'Never, never do that, Mr Murray. The walls at the back of the Embassy are patrolled by security personnel with huge, fierce wolf-hounds. They would tear you to pieces instantly!'

I had never ever caught a glimpse of them or heard them, but this night of blood-curdling howling confirmed their presence. The noise subsided. What had started the wolf-hounds off I was never able to discover, but it was very disturbing and neither Nora nor I could sleep, so she made some coffee and we sat silently, both waiting for we knew not what. Sure enough, before the hour had passed, the wail of an air-raid siren sounded.

'That's an air-raid warning,' I told Nora. 'Stay here while I go and see what it's all about.' I rushed out into the garden and made for the main Embassy building. I met one of the Chancellery servants shepherding Sir Stafford's personal staff – the butler and maids – through a door on the side of the building, leading to the cellars.

'What's up?' I asked him.

'The Germans are attacking Russia!' he said, dramatically. 'You'd better get inside.'

I rushed back to the cottage to tell Nora the news. She took it quite calmly and flatly refused to join the others, saying she would stay in the cottage and wait for me. I went to my office in the main building to await the arrival of my chief. It was not long before all the Service Attachés arrived. Everyone knew the Germans were about to attack Russia, but we had no details as to when and were awaiting instructions from London. The 'All Clear' sounded and later, in the early hours of that morning, military music began blaring through all the public loudspeakers in Moscow. Then came the first official announcement over radio and loudspeakers, made by Molotov, denouncing the treachery of Hitler and the fascist bandits, and then telling us what the glorious armies of the Soviet would do to them. But as the day wore on, the most important thing to us was Churchill's speech offering the hand of friendship and help to the Soviet Union. This was wonderful news, and when I got home and explained to Nora what was happening, I said that surely now the NKVD would not persecute her, as we were now all friends.

The days, then weeks passed swiftly by. It was a case of eat, sleep and work in one continuous routine. The question of Nora's presence in my cottage seemed to have been forgotten, and though our relationship with the Soviet was that of allies, I would still not allow Nora to leave the Embassy grounds. In the Embassy itself there was nothing but feverish activity. The arrival of the 'hush-hush' visitors, Churchill, Lord Beaverbrook and their staff, was chewed over with bated breath by the lower echelons of the Embassy personnel who were actually given very little official information. Nevertheless, we knew what was going on. One day Sir Stafford sent me to the Kremlin with a personal note for Molotov. I felt quite thrilled at the thought of going inside the Kremlin, which was not very far from the Embassy and could easily be seen across the Moscow Canal, which ran parallel with the *Sofiyskaya naberezhnaya*. I was driven there in the Ambassador's Rolls Royce – the first time I had ever ridden in one. Although it was very ancient and the bodywork well-worn, it was like riding on an air-cushion. It must, however, have been twenty years old. Much to my disappointment, we were not allowed beyond the portals. A smart uniformed officer came out and after I had verified that he was the proper person to receive the document, we returned to the Embassy.

In August 1941, the Thirtieth Military Mission, headed by Lieut-General Sir Noel Mason-MacFarlane arrived. With him were Vice-Admiral Miles, Air Vice-Marshal Collier, Group Captain Bird, and a Colonel Exham – a brass-hat who represented the CIGS (Chief of the Imperial General Staff), each with their various staffs. The main body of the Mission was meanwhile being established in the ice-free northern part of Murmansk and the White Sea port of Archangel that was more or less frozen in during the winter.

After several weeks had elapsed and the Mission was really getting under way, Sir Stafford Cripps called me in and informed me that although I would still be serving the Foreign Office, I was to be seconded personally to Lieut-General MacFarlane. I was very pleased about this, and had, in fact, been making myself as useful as I could in many small ways to members of the Mission staff. Mac-Farlane was, to me, not only a high-ranking soldier, but he was what I called 'a man's man' in every way. There was no stuck-uppiness about him in his dealings with the ordinary staff. He looked and acted every inch like a soldier. He stood well over six foot and was as broad as an ox. He called me in after my interview with Sir Stafford and told me I was to write up his War Diary. This was extremely confidential, and there would be one original which he would send to London, and one copy which would be retained by Sir Stafford. This was to be one of my special duties and under no circumstances was to be discussed. I found him a very considerate chief. The diary write-up was one of the jobs previously done by Colonel Exham who had been seconded to MacFarlane by the War Office.

There is one anecdote that I would like to relate concerning my new chief. It always makes me smile when I recollect it, especially as it gives some idea of what the Russians at that time thought to be right and proper.

Sir Noel, as a true Scot, always wore his kilt and sporran. A discreet intimation was one day passed on from the Kremlin that the Russians thought it was not very becoming for a man to be seen wearing a skirt as it offended the moral ethics of the Russian people. For the rest of his stay, he wore the regulation army trousers.

The Germans through their conquest of Norway had been able to establish air bases at its most northerly tip and Murmansk was already suffering from the attentions of the Luftwaffe, to which the Russians had no answer. Although we were in a very tight position ourselves it was nevertheless decided to sacrifice an air squadron from our own meagre forces to help the Russians. As there were no air bases in Murmansk, Group Captain Bird was sent there to work with the Russians on the details for building one. The place was mapped out and the Russians said they would have it ready within two months. Group Captain Bird returned from his trip, tired, unshaven, and a visibly shaken man. He gave me his notes and asked me to type out his report in time to catch the courier plane leaving for England the next day. I worked all night on the report, and had it ready for him by six in the morning. He was so grateful; he did not know how to thank me enough, especially as he received a commendation from the Chief of Air Staff. Bird told me confidentially he did not think the Russians would be able to do the job, especially in the time stipulated. He said the Russians had absolutely no equipment of any kind to do it with and their only labour force was comprised of thousands of ill-nourished, under-fed political prisoners and the site they had picked was all forest.

But the RAF 171 Wing of Hurricanes arrived on schedule and an air base, of a sort, was already completed by that time. Bird later told me that the trees had been hacked down by hand. Prisoners in their thousands had been put to work on it and those that fell from sheer exhaustion and or died were simply left where they fell and pounded underfoot with the ice and snow that formed the runways. 171 Wing did their job and earned the grudging admiration of the Russians, who were very sparse in praise of anything we did for them. After a while, the planes were taken over by the Russians themselves.

We were meanwhile receiving a stream of reports from Intelligence in London, detailing the appalling losses the Russians were suffering and the extent of the German advances. We were supplying the Russians, too, with reports from our Intelligence Service on dispositions and movements of the enemy. But they would not reciprocate by giving us information from their side. A tight silence was maintained by the Russians. MacFarlane tried by every means possible to visit the battle fronts, but he was side-stepped and blocked at every turn. Later, much later, he was allowed to visit one battlefront but it was not one of the important ones.

The naval side of the Mission had a much better reception from the Russians. This was evident to me later, when I was in Archangel.

Shortly after the Murmansk report, I was asked by Vice-Admiral Miles if I would do the report of one of his submarine commanders who had acted as an observer on one of the Russian submarines during an action in the Black Sea. It was another all-night rush job for me which I completed satisfactorily. I do not think I will be breaking any Security Act when I mention that the report praised the high standards of efficiency and discipline among the Russian crew; even when the submarine, following a successful action, was constantly depth-charged and damaged, they still maintained their high morale. He also found them friendly, though guardedly so.

By this time, it was already August. A new 'Hush' machine had arrived from England – it was a 'Code Scrambler'. This chattered away frantically, churning out messages at a fantastic rate. Certain of the messages, however, we still had to decode manually. It appeared there were only two other machines like it in the whole world – one in London and the other in Washington. With it came an Army Signals Corps Group headed by a Captain, who was soon installed in our cipher room. It was then that my chief summoned me and explained that the Mission with the arrival of the Signals' personnel were having accommodation problems. He wanted to know if I would give up the cottage in the Embassy gardens and return to Bagshawe's old place. If I consented to do this, it would be possible to quarter the Signals staff in my cottage, which would be more convenient for them as the Scrambler had to function day and night. I agreed, and transport was provided for all my things. Nora, of course, came with me and, like me, was quite pleased about the change. She would be seeing Rebecca again with whom she had been quite friendly and so would have someone to talk to.

All the senior staff of the Mission had been quartered in the former Yugoslav Embassy, where they were well looked after by the Russians who had turned it into a kind of hotel. I had occasion to visit there on quite a number of times in the course of my duties. It was run by Gabaridze, the Maître d'Hôtel from the Metropole Hotel. It was he who arranged the menus and I had many sumptuous meals there. The thing I enjoyed most was the Caviar and real black Russian bread. Very few of the Mission cared about Caviar and there were always four huge bowls of it containing about two pounds each on the dining table at lunch-time. I used to waffle about a quarter of a pound of it at each sitting. My mouth always waters when I think of it. The Russians also supplied a fleet of the large black 'Zis' cars with chauffeurs to provide transport to and from the Embassy for our staff.

After Nora and I were comfortably installed in *Maly kharitonevsky*, Vice-Admiral Miles asked me if I could put up one of his staff, a young naval writer who had had a bad time coming over from England. It appeared that his mate had been killed right next to him on the ship bringing him over. Group Captain Bird also asked me if I could put up one of his Flight Sergeants. This youngster had arrived in Moscow to a tumultuous reception from the Russian populace as he appeared with his head, face, and hands swathed in bandages. They thought he had been wounded by the Germans. In actual fact, on arrival in Archangel he had been badly bitten by mosquitos with resultant blood poisoning! Then Sir Noel asked me if I could put up his Quartermaster Sergeant. Having plenty of room in the house, and the adjoining archivist's flat being empty, I took them all in, and this made good company for everyone.

Not long after this, we had our first air raid in Moscow. It is a night I shall never forget for quite a number of reasons.

I was on duty. It was about ten-thirty p.m. I was in the Cipher Room with three of the Signals staff busy decoding. The Captain in charge lay stretched out on a couch in the corner fast asleep, having just finished a long spell on duty. A terrific explosion shook the building. We heard the roar of a bomber passing overhead. Following the explosion there was a heavy dull thud in the distance.

One of the signallers said quietly, 'That's Jerry; he's passing overhead. There's generally a stick of five – that's two gone – I hope to Christ the next will miss us!'

There was another shaking thud, this time from a distance. We sat quite still waiting for the explosion, when it came it was in the distance.

'They've missed us!' the signaller said. But even as he spoke there came the sound of a whole series of light thuds. Just then the Captain woke up and groggily got to his feet.

'Air raid, eh? Carry on. I'll go and look around.' With that he unbolted the French windows that led out into the garden and disappeared. We continued working. After a while he re-appeared with an armful of incendiary bombs. They were aluminium clad cylinders, about fifteen inches high; he'd got six of them. He staggered over to our table and stood them up in a row, saying, 'Here's a present from Germany,' went back to the couch, fell on it, and was fast asleep again.

We eyed the incendiaries warily, but carried on with our job. None of us dared touch them, because we did not know anything about them. In the meantime, we heard a lot of shouting and banging going on in the building. We carried on until our scrambler stopped, and then I decided to go out and have a look. In the main hall were two huge supporting pillars. Hugging one of them closely with outstretched arms, was one of our Chancellery servants. He was a Cockney.

'What on earth are you doing?' I asked.

'Well, it's like this 'ere. If a bomb drops that-a-way, I slides round 'ere. If it falls this-a-way, I slides round the other side, see?'

I couldn't help laughing, as I made my way to the front door. On the steps outside sat the General and several of the Mission staff – they were all begrimed with soot. It appeared that the Embassy had been hit with incendiaries and they'd all been on the roof putting the fires out. There was also a thick pall of dust hanging in the air which was making everyone cough – the Kremlin Walls just beyond the canal, facing the Embassy had been hit, so filling the air with the centuries-old dust from the brickwork. I was told the bomber had passed overhead letting loose a stick of bombs, one of which had blown up a building to the rear of the Embassy. One had fallen by the front gates but had not exploded – a bomb-disposal squad were working on it. A third had hit and gone right through the canal bridge without exploding. A fourth had fallen by the Kremlin Wall and also had not exploded, and we had sent a couple of our bomb-disposal experts to deal with that. The fifth bomb had actually landed on the Kremlin Wall and had exploded. Hence the heavy pall of dust and smoke which now enveloped the Embassy.

Sir Stafford Cripps' butler now appeared on the scene and the General sent him to get something for them to drink. He appeared shortly with several bottles of Sir Stafford's best wine. He was so nervous, he had forgotten to open the bottles or bring glasses. The General just took them off him, knocked the top of the bottles off on the stone steps and poured the wine into the cupped hands of his colleagues, got one of them to do the same for him and that's how they refreshed themselves. After picking up all the news, I mentioned we'd got some incendiaries on our desk in the cipher room and then went back to work and tell the others what had happened. Shortly afterwards, one of the bomb disposal chaps came in and took the incendiaries away. He said that there was no need to have been frightened as they had already been expertly defused. The Captain still lay fast asleep, quite unconscious of what had been happening around him. I wish he'd told us that he had rendered them harmless before passing out. It would have saved us a lot of worry. The expert told us that two of our bomb-disposal chaps who had gone over to the Kremlin to help the Russians to deal with their bomb had returned scared out of their wits. They had found the Russians sitting astride a thousand-pounder stolidly pounding away with a cold chisel and hammer at the bomb in an attempt to defuse it. It appeared they had very little equipment. They would not let our chaps touch it and finally completed the job, only taking their advice on its mechanism.

At midnight, I was relieved by my colleague, Jimes, and was

driven home, glad to get back. I rushed into the house expecting to be greeted by Nora who always waited up for my return. Not seeing her I rushed into the bedroom calling her name. The bedroom was empty and there was no answer to my call! I had a sudden feeling of apprehension as I dashed around the rooms searching for her. I woke up the young Air Force Sergeant and my two other guests in turn. They had come back to the house at various hours during the evening, but none of them had remembered seeing her. I felt my fears rising. At that moment the telephone bell rang. I rushed to the phone wondering who'd be ringing at such a late hour. It was Jimes.

'Listen, John, I've some strange news for you. I've just had a telephone call put through to me. It was from your Nora. She sounded terrified. All she could say was that she was being held at the sixty-sixth Police Uchastok (the district precinct). Tell John, she said and then the line went dead.'

As I listened, I felt a dreadful feeling of sickness overtaking me, my legs wobbled, I could only gasp. Dimly I heard Jimes' voice continuing, 'Sorry, old chap, it looks as if our old friends the YMCA have got your Nora. If there's anything I can do, let me know, John.'

I could only mutter, 'The bastards. I'll murder them!'

At that moment I did not know what to do. I was stunned and sick. I went to the cupboard and got a bottle of whisky, opened it and gulped down a couple of swigs, and began to think.

Vasily! Surely he must know something about it. Without more ado I dashed over to the porter's lodge. Vasily was seated at a table with three of the shuttle-service chauffeurs. He looked startled as I rushed up to him shouting, 'Why didn't you tell me about Nora? What's happened to her?' I grabbed him by the shoulder shaking him. He seemed very confused.

'But, Mr Murray, I know nothing, really I don't. All I know is that this evening two men called at the gates and asked to see her. I didn't let them in but called Nora to them. She spoke with them and then they went away. I don't know what they talked about, and Nora afterwards came back and went out herself. I don't know anything more,' he concluded plaintively.

I turned to the chauffeurs, waving my bottle of whisky in the air, 'Come,' I shouted. 'Who'll drive me to the sixty-sixth Police Uchastok? The police there have arrested my wife. I'm going to get her out!' I looked round. Their faces had a sullen, set expression. I knew it was hopeless. All these men were handpicked by the NKVD. They were definitely not going to get entangled with their masters! I groaned in despair. I'd no idea where the Police Headquarters were, and knew that there was no way of finding it, and time was precious.

Then, all of a sudden, several things happened at once. The sirens started again and at the same time a tremendous barrage of anti-aircraft started up. The very building seemed to dance. I had never heard such intensity of gun-fire before. The London barrages that I was to hear later, had nothing on this. It flashed through my mind how the Russians had demanded more anti-aircraft guns from our Military Mission, and here was a barrage going on that would have put any air defence to shame. It was fantastic! Then the door burst open and in stepped another chauffeur. He was huge – a bear of a man, with a big smile on his broad Russian features. He had had to bend down to enter the doorway. He looked askance at us all. Without giving him time to say anything, I turned to him, and still waving my bottle of whisky in the air, implored of him – 'Will you drive me to the sixty-sixth Uchastok? My wife is there. They have arrested her. She is my Russian wife. I love her. Do you understand? I'm British. I'm from the Embassy!'

He gave me a searching glance, there was a pause, then he said in a deep voice, '*Da, da, ya pomogu!*' (Yes, yes, I'll help!) He turned round to the others, the smile gone, his lips curled into a sneer and said something very quickly which I could not catch. Then turning to me said simply, 'Come.' Before we went out I proffered him the bottle.

'Here,' I said. 'Have a drink of this.'

He took a couple of gulps, and his face lit up in a most beauteous smile. He'd such a terrific homely face, it was like a ray of sunshine coming suddenly into my life. He offered the bottle back to me with one hand and thumped his massive chest with the other and boomed, 'By God! That's some drink!'

'Keep it!' I said, 'and put it in your pocket.'

This time he treated the rest of them to a triumphant smile, pocketed the bottle, and went out. The barrage was still on. Lumps of metal were sizzling all around us from the exploding shells. Several windows had already been broken. They were lethal, but by some unexplained miracle, we were not hit. As we drove to the police station, I told him how I had fallen in love with a beautiful Russian girl who loved me, and how the NKVD for no reason at all were persecuting her. I asked wasn't it a shame? Here was me helping Russia, when I could be doing better things, and all the NKVD could do was to make my life a misery. He was of course under the NKVD himself, but I had long ago learnt that there were Russians and Russians, and what I called the real Russians were the most kind-hearted and sensitive people one could ever come across.

We arrived at the police station and I dashed in, followed by the chauffeur, and strode straight to the room marked Chief of the District Police. The chief, a podgy pasty-faced individual was sitting at a table covered with forms and documents. He glanced up with a look of surprise on his face as I walked up to his desk, showing him my passport.

'I'm John Murray, an Englishman from the British Embassy. You have my wife, Nora Korzhenko, here. I've come to take her away.'

He ignored my proffered passport and stared at me with a deliberately insulting sneer. 'Get out of my office. I don't know what you're talking about. There is no Korzhenko here. Go!'

That was enough for me. 'Who do you think you're talking to, you lying son of a bitch, you lying . . .' and I let loose all the Russian swear words and invectives I knew. I'd never used swear words before and never have since, but this was the one time I was in a white-hot rage. 'You – you, devil. How dare you lie to me?' and as I swore I leant over his table and drew my arm back to give him a back-handed swipe that would have blasted him into eternity. He shrank back. Two policemen rushed into the room and stood on either side of him awaiting instructions. At the same time I was gripped by the shoulder and spun aside. It was the chauffeur.

'Softly, softly, *gospodin*, stay, stay,' he boomed at me. I wriggled away and went back to the desk and thumped it with my fist.

'Don't you ever dare lie to me, you dog!' I shouted. His face assumed a puce colour, he was so taken aback, he did not know what to say. The police in Moscow are always used to dealing with abject, cringing wretches who are in fear and terror of them, and it must have shaken him to have someone address him in the way I did.

He lifted up a hand placatingly, 'Wait a minute. I'll try and find something out for you.'

With that, followed by his henchmen, he retired to a back room. Some twenty minutes passed and still he did not reappear. I was stamping up and down, smoking one cigarette after another. My chauffeur just stood placidly there, occasionally shaking his head and also smoking the meanwhile.

I was just reaching that boiling point when I thought I'd start smashing things up, when two comical looking individuals scuttled in; with their absurdly long black overcoats and pointed shoes sticking out from underneath, their trilby hats squashed well down over their ears, there was no mistaking who they were. They went straight through to the back room. Another fifteen minutes passed and the inspector came back into the room. He was most apologetic. Yes, citizeness Korzhenko was in the building but she had to be kept to have her documents put in order, and if I would go away quietly, she would be sent home in the morning. But I wasn't having that at any price. Now that I knew she was definitely in the building, I was determined to get her away. As far as I was concerned there would be no let-up.

I launched into another paroxysm of invective and as the two NKVD men sidled to the door to see what was going on, I took off my coat, flung it among all the papers on the desk, and stated that I was not going away without her. Furthermore, I said that if I had any more nonsense from him, I would go back to my Embassy and ring up Gospodin Stalin personally and complain of their treatment of me.

As I was saying all this, the towering figure of the chauffeur came up beside me and nodding his massive head kept on booming out interjections, such as 'Yes, listen to him, he's a Minister of the Great Britain! Yes, he's got much power! Be careful what you say to him!'

The things he was saying were so ludicrous that under any other circumstances I would have laughed my head off, but his manner made him look like Jupiter admonishing his lesser gods.

The inspector's face had by this time turned an ashen-grey colour. Then he motioned to the two NKVD men to go into the back room and they went into another pow-wow. Meanwhile I was again pacing up and down smoking cigarette after cigarette, boiling up internally, fit to burst.

I'd nearly reached the end of my tether, what with fear and anger, when the side doors opened. There stood Nora blinking in the unaccustomed light, held by the arm on one side by a tough looking policewoman. Nora's face was bruised and puffed; her eyelids were swollen with crying. As soon as she made me out standing there, she tore herself away and rushed into my arms.

'Oh, John——' was all she could say, and leant her head on my shoulders, her body trembling and heaving as she sobbed. The surprised look of disbelief that suddenly flashed across her face when she first recognised me was one that I will never forget. The inspector and the two stooges had meanwhile silently entered. I looked enquiringly over Nora's head, thinking there would be some sort of document to sign.

'Go, go, go now; go right away!' He gestured with his hand.

We turned and left, the chauffeur leading and I following with my arms round Nora. At the door I stopped and looking back spat out, 'Tell your people if they ever lay hands on my wife again, I'll kill them!' and I meant every word I said.

We got back to the house. I slipped another bottle of whisky from my precious store into Ivan Ivanovitch's hands and thanked him for his help. He patted me on the shoulder, 'I was glad to help, be careful, and God bless you both.' Such was the heart of this Russian.

Back in the warmth and security of our home, Nora told me what had happened. Vasily had come that evening to tell her two strangers were at the gate and they had some news for her concerning her passport. She had gone to the gate and they had told her in a friendly manner that owing to the new regulations, all Russians had to register for food ration cards, and she would get hers if she went to the district police station despite the fact her passport was not in order, that this in fact would be restored to her, now she was living with Russia's Allies.

Overjoyed, she had later set out to go to the police station. When she had reached the end of the street, a black car had drawn up alongside her. The same two men had sprung out and bundled her into the car. They drove to the station where she was put into a room and told she was under arrest. At that moment the air raid sirens began to wail and the anti-aircraft guns began to go off. There was instant confusion. Seeing the telephone, she dialled the Embassy and was put through to Jimes. She managed to speak a few words when the door opened and a policewoman rushed in and tore the telephone from her. She was then stripped and searched. Her ring and wrist-watch were taken from her and her passport was doubly cancelled with another black streak. When she tried to speak, she was struck across the face and told to shut up, and that as soon as the raid was over she would be transported to the Lubyanka prison. This was Russia's most notorious prison for political offenders; few who passed through its doors ever came out alive.

She had then been taken down the steps to a cell where the only other occupant was a prostitute. There was no light and they had to keep moving about because of the rats that kept scuttling around. She had lost track of time and had given up hope of ever seeing me again. When the policewoman had unlocked the cell door and ordered her to accompany her, she had thought this was the end. When she came to the part of telling me how she felt when she recognised me standing in that room, she broke down and could say no more. I comforted her as best as I could and reminded her softly what the cards had foretold. 'See,' I said, 'they never lie!' I couldn't think of anything more to say. It took Nora a couple of days to get over the shock. That night I hugged her closer than ever, vowing I'd never let her go.

Next morning I made a point of going to the Yugoslav house and getting Gabaridze on my side. I knew the chauffeur would be in for big trouble and I wanted to do everything I could to shield him. I told Gabaridze the story and said I hoped no harm would come to Ivan Ivanovitch for helping me, that he was a true Russian with the kind of heart that I so admired.

'Real Russians like that are the backbone of your country, and it makes me proud to help such people. While there are such brave men in Russia, there is no fear of the Germans being able to conquer them!' Then I added, 'I'm sure even the NKVD would not harm such a man, so brave and filled with true human kindness!'

Gabaridze took it all in. I'd guessed he was quite an important man himself in the NKVD.

He told me they were sad times these days. Not long ago his wife had died and he had not even been able to get permission for leave to go home and arrange the funeral. His only son was a soldier at the front and the bad news, which he knew about – the Russian defeats which the Russian public was kept ignorant of, made him greatly fear for the safety of his son. I commiserated with him.

I was glad to see Ivan Ivanovitch still doing service as a chauffeur. He avoided me and I knew that he'd been put on the rack, from his pale appearance and sober manner. The main point however was that he had not 'disappeared'.

Some time after this event I fell ill. It all began with a temperature, headache, and vomiting, then diarrhoea. At first I thought it was from overwork and catching a chill through the long nights of duty. Eventually, I had to stay at home, unable to carry on any longer. Jimes came to see me and said he would report my sickness to the Embassy. He said everything was now chaotic there. I reassured him I would soon get well. But I didn't. Things got worse and worse. Nora did everything for me – washed and bathed me, but the illness was so severe and took such a rapid turn that Nora became frightened. With the diarrhoea I was now passing flesh and blood from my intestines and lost weight alarmingly. I told Nora that I thought I was dying. My one worry was what would happen to her. One afternoon while I was in a semi-coma, she slipped out of the house without telling me, and went to search for an old family doctor who'd once served in the Kremlin. She managed by some means or other to find him and explained what had happened to me. He told her to go home and he would call. He came that very evening. A little white-haired fellow whose face was lined with care. He examined me. The first thing he asked for was a glass of warm water in which he put some crystals. I asked him what they were; he said *angliysky sol* (which meant Epsom Salts). Well, I thought, this is the end, Epsom Salts! Why, I'd nothing more to pass through me except my intestines. But he was firm. I had to drink the Salts and then lots of boiled water. You can imagine what happened to me!

He went away and returned some hours later with a small conical sealed glass in which was some yellow liquid. He broke off the top and poured it into a tumbler and made me drink it, gave Nora a couple of tablets to give to me sometime later, and then said he had to leave. He told Nora that that was all he could do. I had a virulent type of dysentry and he had given me a bacterial solution to combat it. Whether I recovered was in the hands of God. If I was to feel better later, she was to feed me at first on nothing but the water from boiled rice and later the whites only of lightly boiled eggs, until my stomach healed. He said she was not to worry too much as I was a healthy and strong young man and should get over it. I really thought that my days were numbered. But gradually, through Nora's care and devotion, I began to pull round. That doctor had saved my life. Nora would not let anyone but herself prepare my food. Two and a half weeks later, I was on my feet again, a little thin and wobbly, but increasing rapidly in strength.

It was on 15 September, 1941, that I resumed my duties at the Embassy were further complicated by the arrival, at the end of broken the Russian Lines and were preparing for their advance on Moscow. Irrespective we still worked on. The difficulties of the Embassy were further complicated by the arrival at the end of September, of a Trades Union delegation headed by Sir Walter Citrine. Shortly after their arrival I was summoned to Mr Dunlop's office. He informed me that the whole of the Embassy and Mission staff were to be evacuated temporarily to Kuibyshev, and my flat and belongings had to be left in charge of the servants I designated for this purpose. I filled out the form there and then in his office, naming Nora Korzhenko, Rebecca and Vasily as the custodians. He accepted it without a word.

When I returned home that evening to Nora, I explained what was happening and pointed out it would be too dangerous for her to go with me as once outside the house I could not protect her, but as long as she stayed and was regarded officially as the person responsible for my property, no one could touch her. I said it was bound to be only a temporary evacuation as I was firmly convinced in spite of what everyone said, that Moscow would not be taken. It was a hard decision, but she agreed that it was the right one. The next day, 9 October, the Embassy staff got official notice of the evacuation. General MacFarlane said I was to be issued with an Army uniform to wear. So I was given a battledress. It was too big, but Nora worked on it to make it a better fit. It was quite damp with tears when I tried it on. The next day was simply pandemonium getting everything ready at the Embassy. I went back home in the afternoon and was told to await the Army lorry that was to take me to the station.

I learned that General MacFarlane had also to leave Moscow in spite of protesting vigorously that he preferred to remain. Several members of the American Embassy staff, however, were permitted to remain – America at that time still being a neutral country, and as during the Norwegian invasion, would look after British interests. Finding out that my old acquaintance, Reinhardt, would be one of those staying, I contacted him and asked him to keep an eye on Nora for me and help her all he could as she was more to me than just my housekeeper. This he promised to do – a promise that he fulfilled as I was later to learn. Nora, of course, was very sad and tearful as the time approached for me to leave. Now I still had the small figurine of my Madonna, I had carried it around with me wherever I'd been, in Finland during the Finno–Russian war; in Sweden; in Norway, during my escape, and I had brought it with me to Moscow. It had always been a kind of mascot to me.

I gave it to Nora and said as long as she kept it with her, no harm could befall her. The lorry, an open truck, arrived about seven that evening. The young naval rating and I climbed into it. A last tearful farewell to Nora and a goodbye to Rebecca and Vasily, and off we went to the Embassy. There the Cipher Scrambler was loaded on to it, a rifle with no ammunition was handed to each of us and our truck set off for the station. Arriving at the station, which was jammed at the entrance with troops and lorries in ever-increasing numbers, we were told our train was not ready and that we were to park at a spot some distance away from the station in order to avoid getting entangled with the mounting traffic. We found the place and settled down to wait. It was now about ten. The night was dark and damp, drizzle and sleet were falling. We stomped up and down in the open truck to keep warm. An unending stream of lorries of all types were passing us. Some were filled with troops, mostly young men with weather-tanned faces. They were warmly clad in greatcoats or three-quarter padded tunics, with the usual thick round helmet hats that could be let down to provide ear and neck mufflers. They looked in superb physical condition, well-fed and well-built.

In contrast, some lorries were filled with civilians, mostly women, shawls on their heads, clad in heavy drab coats, women with grim determined faces, only a few men but quite a number of young teenagers full of chatter and restless movement. They were the same type of youngsters that I had noted during the air raids. They would be on the roof-tops during an attack, dancing up and down, skipping across from roof-top to roof-top, shouting and gesticulating to one another, quite oblivious of the danger, and enjoying every moment.

Such was the cavalcade that passed us on their way to the Moscow front. After three hours, we received notice to return to the Kazan Station, and I soon found myself in the welcome warmth of one of the carriages, sharing a compartment with the young naval rating, Jimes and two of the army personnel. After a further delay of about an hour owing to another air raid, our train steamed slowly out of the station, destination Kuibyshev. That journey of some five hundred miles, normally a twenty-four hour trip, took five days. There were constant stoppages en route. Some to arrange food for our hungry party, which had left Moscow without loading the provisions that had been stacked up in the Embassy main hall specially for this purpose. Everybody blamed everybody else. The young naval rating remarked, 'It's just like the Pongos!' A remark that nearly caused a fight in our compartment, but after all, the military personnel of the Mission were responsible.

The Russians fed us from their meagre food supplies. It consisted mostly of rye bread and cabbage soup of an indeterminate colour. Luckily for Sir Stafford and some of his very senior staff, the American Ambassador and those of his staff travelling with him shared their food with them, they having had the foresight to see that they were well-provided with rations before they started. The Trades Union delegation also travelled with us, having hardly had any time to confer with their Russian counterparts. In any case, their arrival had served the purpose of window-dressing which was most essential.

The most outstanding event I can recall from that journey was a scene at one of the marshalling yards through which we passed. I looked through the window and saw a stationary string of goods wagons, some open, others vans with partly opened doors. The open wagons were piled with machinery, transmission shafts and wheels, machine frames, huge electric motors; and sitting among them were women workers in their thickly padded jackets with shawls over their heads, all dappled with snow, and huddled together for warmth. Their faces were a grey putty colour, their eyes sunken deep in their sockets. They showed no sign of interest in our train passing them by. There was no animation or movement among them. They could have been frozen corpses for all I knew.

Eventually we arrived at Kuibyshev and were mostly quartered in one of the newest co-operative buildings. It was quite large. We slept and worked in this building which was situated on a main road that led down to the Volga. The river was of immense breadth and the opposite bank seemed to fade into the mist. It was a bright, sunny, cold day when I first set eyes on the River Volga and it made a wonderful picture, with huge ships in full sail and barges ploughing through its waters, which were still unfrozen.

Work was still hectic and as the news we were handling grew in seriousness, my mind often went back to Nora and how I could get in touch with her. But communication was impossible. Moscow was virtually surrounded by that time. I had only been in Kuibyshev two weeks when I got the shock of my life. Air Vice-Marshal Collier called me in to his office and told me the Mission had decided to send me home for reasons of health! I had recovered from the bout of dysentry and was feeling fine in myself, although outwardly I may have shown some effects of the illness. The arrangements were made; I was to fly to Archangel with the Trades Union delegation and certain of the Military Mission personnel, and a visiting journalist, Mrs Huxley.

Our flight was fixed for the following day, 23 October, 1941, at the ungodly hour of four a.m. The plane was a converted Russian two-engined bomber. The machine gun under the roof blister had been removed. There was a long table in the centre of the plane, with a continuous bench seating all round the interior. The pilot and radio-navigator sat in the front nose of the plane. All the luggage was loaded and also four small wooden cases that had seals upon them. They were about three feet long by one foot square, made of thick timber. It took two men to lift one, they were that heavy. The Embassy Secretary who was seeing me off, told me that they contained about three-and-a-half million pounds worth of platinum that Stalin was sending to England with the Trades Union delegation as a gift from Russia for our aircraft engine industry.

It was quite dark when we flew off. The plane flew quite steadily and I could get up and walk about and peer over the heads of the pilot and navigator through the nose of the plane. After four hours of flying we reached Gorky where a Russian delegation of Trades Union officials with an interpreter awaited us at the airfield to drive us into the town itself. The Mission personnel stayed behind, but the journalist, Mrs Huxley, and myself went with the Trades Union. First we had a good solid breakfast, and afterwards were taken to the Gorky Motor Works where we were shown the Russian war effort. It was only a quick, cursory look around and afterwards we were soon gathered together to be taken back to the plane.

It was then discovered that one of the Trades Union delegates was missing. This caused a great deal of upset among the Russians and their interpreter was so upset she could hardly speak. So I did the interpreting. We found the missing chap, all innocence, toddling down a road to look at a church building. Neither he nor the rest of the delegates could understand the fuss. They were so naïve and ignorant of how life was conducted in Russia, that to me it was unbelievable! They still had the starry-eyed belief that it was a free, democratic country, where people could live normal uninterrupted lives. I think they even believed they were dealing with genuine Trade Unionist counterparts. They did not realise that if anything had happened to one of our party, the whole of our so-called Trades Union hosts and the interpreter, could have been liquidated without even a trial.

I had to do a great deal of explaining to the Russians to convince them that it had been a harmless and innocent mistake, but some members of the Trades Union still thought it a huge joke.

Finally, we were all shepherded on to the plane again, which had in the meantime been refuelled. It was about noon when we took off on the last lap of our non-stop flight to Archangel. We flew for seven hours on this lap, flying just a few hundred feet off the ground. We seemed to be flying for hour after hour through a lane in the midst of a vast unending forest. In actual fact, we were following the railway cutting of the line Moscow-Vologda-Archangel and had to fly low to avoid enemy planes.

It was about seven p.m. that same day when we landed on the ice-covered airfield at Archangel. It was the darkest, coldest, most unfriendly place I had ever arrived at. As soon as all the baggage was off the plane several cars drove up and we were surrounded by a very friendly group of Russian Trade delegates who said that a special official evening supper had been prepared for our party. Just as I was about to step into a car, a little short busy-looking member of our own Trades Union delegation told me that I was not included in the invitation as it was only meant for them. The Military Mission staff had already gone with some of the others – I think the upset in Gorky had something to do with this because I had been somewhat outspoken at the time. The Russians looked a bit puzzled when I did not go with them, but I didn't enlighten them. They all drove off and I stood for a while taking in the scene.

There was nothing in sight except our lone plane standing on the snow-covered airfield. The airport was just a large low-roofed building made of wood consisting of one huge hall, surrounded by a few small offices and a Radio room. A couple of uniformed offi-cers were eyeing me speculatively. I went up to them, showed them my passport and explained that I wanted transport to the town of Archangel where I would be staying at the Intourist House. Within a short time they produced for me a horse-driven sleigh and soon I was bounding along over the ice and snow with a big warm fur rug wrapped tightly round me and only the tip of my nose exposed to the wind. Over and over again the thought went through my mind, 'What the hell am I doing here, in this Godforsaken dump?' Nora was constantly in my mind. I felt I was being drawn along a path to which I had no affinity. I couldn't think clearly. I was aware only of a hopeless, helpless sense of tiredness creeping over me. After what seemed ages of sliding, with occasional back-breaking jolts over a desolate wilderness of ice and snow, we gradually approached lanes of small timber buildings, in between which ran a road of packed snow that gradually led to the Intourist building.

Imagine my surprise when, before entering the building, I noticed the four wooden boxes of platinum stacked against the wall outside. I paid off the driver and gave him a packet of cigarettes which I rightly guessed meant more than the money to him. I went to the desk and asked if there were any messages for me. It appeared I was expected; a message had been left for me and a room reserved on the first floor. The message was a note from Lieut. Fisher, RN, who'd first of all been with the Mission in Moscow, and later sent up to Archangel. He was an ASDIC (Anti-submarine devices) expert and the Russians needed his expertise up here against the submarine and acoustic mines menace. He wrote he would be seeing me later on in the evening and that I was not to turn in until he arrived.

I took my things and went up to my room, passing a grim-faced woman seated in the corridor. She was the 'watcher', and as I later found out, seemed to be on duty twenty-four hours a day. She was about forty-five years of age, buxom, dressed in black, with greying hair tightly swept back and formed into a top-knot bun, which all added to her formidable appearance. When I spoke to her in Russian, asking the way to the wash-room, I found I was quite mistaken about her. She brightened up at once and her features assumed quite a homely expression. I had a quick wash under a tap of running cold water which was very refreshing, and then went downstairs to the restaurant. The place was full, mostly of Officers and Captains from the various ships lying in Archangel. There was also a sprinkling of some of the Military Mission's Ordnance Corps soldiers, a couple of whom I recognised had been in Moscow at the time of the first arrival of the Mission personnel.

My biggest surprise, however, was to see Gabaridze striding forward to greet me. It was like meeting an old friend. He told me the Yugoslav house had been closed down with the evacuation of Moscow, and he had been sent up to organise a special hotel and club for all the foreign crews of the ships that were beginning to come in. He would also be running the Intourist House, which was used mainly for the Russian officers and officials from the labour camps in the vicinity. He immediately set about getting me a decent meal. When that was over, I got up and went outside to stretch my legs. Still lying outside on the pavement were the neglected cases of platinum. I was shocked and went back into the restaurant and asked two of our Ordnance Corps lads if they would take the cases up to my room. After much puffing and blowing they managed it, asking me if it was lead I'd got in them. Laughingly I said yes, something like that but not quite.

Lieut. Fisher arrived about eleven-thirty that night. He said they had been extremely busy as there was a Destroyer which was due to sail with a crowd of Trades Union blokes. He told me there was a hell of a shemozzle going on downstairs over some boxes that were missing. I smiled, and pulled away the bedspread which I'd used to cover the cases of platinum.

'This is what they're looking for,' I said. 'There's about three-and-a-half million pounds worth of platinum there, which I found lying on the pavement outside unattended!' and then told him the story. 'You'd better nip down and tell 'em it's here!' which he promptly did. Within a matter of seconds, one of the Trades Union members burst into my room demanding to know what right I'd had to touch the stuff. He really went on alarmingly. I thought he was going to have me clapped in irons on the spot. By this time there was a crowd round the door. I cut him short.

'Shut up!' I said. 'Everyone knows me. I'm from the British Embassy. Do *you* want to make a case of this or do you want *me* to make a case of it? This stuff was lying abandoned on the pavement outside for hours. You can thank your lucky stars it was I who turned up.'

That was that. Lieut. Fisher, whose Christian name was Sasha, stayed with me for a couple of hours swapping yarns and before he went told me he would call in the morning to take me to Norwegian House where I was to report to Group Captain Bird who had been appointed Officer in Charge of the Air Mission to Northern Russia. This was unexpected good news as I was very pleased to have the opportunity of meeting him again.

Sasha, by the way, spoke perfect Russian and held quite a high position in the Naval Mission to whom he was extremely useful. He told me that although he and his father were British, he had, like his father, been born in Russia where they had come under the dual nationality law, under which anyone born in Russia was regarded politically as a Soviet Citizen. At the time of the Revolution, the family had been separated and his father had been conscripted by the Bolsheviks as part of their labour force who mended roads. His mother, with little Sasha (he was then only four or five years of age), had undergone untold hardships in their search for him. They had wandered far and wide until by one of those incredible strokes of fortune, they came upon him working by the roadside with a labour gang. Managing to stifle their excitement at the mutual recognition, they had bided their time and one night he joined up with them. They fled south to the Crimea and managed to get away with other refugees, landing eventually in England. He could still remember the terrible experiences they had undergone during those days of flight.

The next morning I saw the Group Captain who told me he was not sending me off, as the destroyer, on which I was supposed to travel, had in fact already left, but would arrange passage for me on one of the ships in the next convoy. As he was very short-handed, he hoped I would be able to help him out. I was glad of the respite, for the fate of Nora was still uppermost in my mind.

My first big job was to make a verbatim report of a Court of Inquiry that was to be held. As I was, amongst other things, the only shorthand-typist available, I could not refuse. Besides which it was pointed out I would receive a special remuneration from the Admiralty for the work. I did this job satisfactorily and was commended by the Mission heads. It dealt with the mysterious and unaccountable disappearance of a Foreign Office diplomatic bag that had been unloaded from one of the ships; a serious matter, and it remained one of the minor unsolved mysteries of the war.

Later on, Group Captain Bird told me, very apologetically, that owing to the fact that I was still attached to the Mission, a special payment could not be sanctioned. I told him not to worry. He was of course anxious to hear all the news I had about Moscow and Kuibyshev. I mentioned the Trades Union incident and we had a good laugh over it. Further, I told him of a private conversation I had had with Sir Walter Citrine on the plane whilst we were flying to Archangel. I had asked Sir Walter what he thought of the chances of Russian survival now that the Germans had reached Moscow and he had answered that he saw no hope for the Russians and that in his opinion they were finished.

I had answered that nobody in official quarters seemed to have a true knowledge of Russia and the Russians and that in my opinion no one was aware of their true strength, and that they would not only defend Moscow, but also eventually defeat the Germans. But he said he knew more than I of the true position and was afraid that this was the end for Russia. Group Captain Bird reckoned I was right but said there was still a long way to go.

Archangel was a terrible dump in my opinion, especially in the winter months when everything froze solid and the cold was intense. From what I could see the whole town appeared to have been built on a raft of logs. The pathways to the buildings, the roads and sidewalks were composed of rough hewn logs. During the spring, summer and autumn months Archangel was one huge swamp. From the paths and roads to the houses one walked on wooden platforms over the morass underneath. Woe betide anyone who fell overboard. The hordes of mosquitos were fantastic and quite virulent as I was later to learn. But winter froze everything into one solid mass, as soon as the snows came. Archangel itself was on the mouth of the river Dvina that flowed upwards, from the south to the north into the White Sea. Its one main road ran parallel with the river mouth and was divided from the sea by a series of low, squat, white stone buildings. The walls of these were of incredible thickness, some two to three feet broad. It was also at this time that I saw the reindeer driven sleighs. The reindeers were in superb condition, a tribute to the care and love bestowed upon them by their owners. The sight of them trotting so pertly down the snow-covered roads and the tinkle of the bells that adorned their harness always gave an unexpected fairyland touch to the winter scene.

There was another aspect to Archangel and its surrounding districts. It had been used as a place of banishment even in Tsarist times. Most of its inhabitants were either exiles or descendants of exiles. Once there, the possibility of escape was minimal. There was only one railway running from it and that was always tightly controlled and the same applied to the ports on the White Sea coast. The surrounding impenetrable forests and swamps were of such vast depth that anyone managing to run away would probably perish. There was, however a kind of free community, that is, exiles among whom were professional people, like doctors, dentists and teachers who lived and formed a mutual aid group that were allowed to exist, but not leave Archangel. They married, bore children, and plied their various professions where and how possible. The officers of the NKVD who watched over them were themselves mostly men who had fallen into disfavour at some time or other and had been relegated to duty there as some kind of punishment.

After my arrival I was kept very busy, which was just as well, as I was in a state of despair and almost crazy with anxiety about Nora. One consolation I found very gratifying: Group Captain Bird's appreciation of my help. As I was on call for all three services on a variety of tasks my time was fully occupied.

In the course of my duties I had occasion to visit one of our ships lying at Molotovsk, one of the new ports constructed in the White Sea, and having some time to spare, wandered through the high stacked blocks of timber to the edge of a broad highway that had been trampled out in the snow. Suddenly to the left of my vision I saw the vanguard of a long line of human beings marching eight or ten abreast guarded on either side by immensely tall heavily-built soldiers, armed with rifles and revolvers strapped round their thick grey long coats. Others had huge wolf-hounds, a pair to each man, straining at their leashes as they marched along. The column seemed to have suddenly erupted from the snow-covered background and it seemed without end. The guards completely ignored me as they occasionally bawled and cursed the prisoners to get a move on. I was a bit anxious but held rooted to the spot as I watched this strange sight.

Instinctively counting, I reckoned there were about 2,000 of them. I was amazed that the guards disregarded me, but it gradually dawned upon me that, dressed as I was in a Russian fur cap, with my fur collared coat of black cloth and leather knee boots, I looked to them like one of the dreaded Commissars from Moscow checking on their behaviour. It was a dark, gloomy winter day, the cold intense and deadening, all around was an unending expanse of snow and ice, with the fringes of a black impenetrable forest in the background. The prisoners I saw were past looking like human beings. Dressed in ragged and patched-up quilted jackets, greasy and stained, held together by bits of string, rope and straps, with legs and feet covered in formless felt knee-boots patched and wrapped round with dirty strips of cloth, they presented a dreadful sight as they shuffled along with stumbling, leaden steps, seemingly unaware of the shouts directed at them.

To me, it was what could be seen of their muffled faces that was so terrible and nightmarish. From under a fantastic array of fur and cloth headgear they appeared as skull-like faces over which layers of grey yellowish skin had been stretched. From out of deep set eye sockets stared glazed, unseeing eyes, with an unforgettable look of hopeless despair. Their heads bobbed up and down with each shuffling step they took, as though it was a supreme effort even to move. Although these were men and women together they were practically quite undistinguishable.

After the column had passed, curious to see where they had come from, I walked in the direction from which they had appeared.

I soon came upon what appeared in the distance to be a wooden lighthouse, it was a watch-tower and on my right, parallel with the highway, I became aware of a steep ditchway that was so deep, the high wooden palisade topped with barbed wire that ran with it was not even discernible from the roadway. Far behind, I could make out endless rows of long wooden huts half buried under the snow. I could detect no movement among them. So desolate and silent was the scene that it was almost as though I had stumbled across some long-dead outpost of the arctic.

I veered away from the scene and quite unexpectedly came upon a shipyard. It was derelict. Something that had been started, left unfinished and neglected. The snow-capped skeletons of wooden stocks seemed incongruous in such a place so I made a quick investigation. Strewn here and there along their length were the hulls of five submarines in various stages of abandoned construction, some almost buried in the snow. The whole lot intermingled with steel plates and wheels long since eaten away with rust. Such an installation did not make sense to me. I wondered what the Russians had been thinking of to set up a naval shipyard in such a desolate area, so far from communications and engineering facilities. It puzzled me at the time. I made some cautious enquiries among the few Russian friends I had made in Archangel. From them it appeared that two years previously, early in 1939, German specialists had arrived from Germany to set up the shipyard. What for, no one knew, except that prison labour had been employed. These specialists I was told, had all packed up and hurriedly gone home two months before the outbreak of war.

Most of the Russian officials with whom we had to deal were quite unco-operative and contrary, and even though we were helping them, they remained suspicious and were always putting difficulties in our way, apart from keeping us well-watched. For instance, when the tanks and guns were unloaded from our ships, the Russians took over at once and our people were not even allowed to touch them. We were not even permitted to set up a hospital for the sick and wounded that arrived with the convoys, which was also a source of friction. The officials we had to deal with were hand-picked men who would never take any decisions unless directed from the very top, which meant their superiors in Moscow.

Some of the Russians, however, were what I call human and one could get on well with them in a guarded sort of way. Gabaridze was one. When I had first arrived he got the small five man orchestra to strike up the popular old First World War marching song, 'It's a long way to Tipperary' as a kind of welcome for me, much to the astonishment of some of our men in the restaurant at the time, who joined in the chorus. It was a terrific hit with the Russians. Later I asked if they would play a real Russian song for me and he chose a piece called 'Suliko', a haunting Caucasian folk melody about a lover who had been turned into a nightingale. It was such a sweet song that I got him to get the orchestra to play it several times for me.

There was a little wizened old man that used to sit drinking alone in the restaurant. I had noticed him several times. One evening I went over to his table and bought him a drink. He was so delighted his gratitude was quite moving; I'd noticed he seemed very sad and dejected. In the course of our conversation he told me a very tragic story. He was Captain of an Esthonian ship bringing the first load of tanks to Russia. Previously he had been on the Atlantic run braving all the perils of the sea. His ship, having been in an English port at the time of the outbreak of the war, had been commandeered for war service. He and his crew, some with their wives, had been quite content to serve under the British flag on the Atlantic war run. They had then been frightened and upset about this, but had been reassured all would be well sailing under the British flag.

Once they had docked and unloaded in Archangel, however, the Russians had put the ship under arrest, claiming it was Soviet property. The Captain and his crew were then hauled before the Russian Authorities (NKVD) and told they must consider themselves as Russian citizens and would not be allowed to leave Russia. Without the Captain explaining, I could well imagine the terror and anxiety this aroused in them. Up till now, they were, however, allowed to live on their boat which was docked further down in a place called Ekonomiya where our Military Mission personnel were stationed and, beyond infrequent calls from a 'politico' officer, were allowed to come and go freely in Archangel. This was no doubt due to pressure exerted by our Military Mission. The main point of his story – they did not mind leaving the ship that had been their livelihood for so many years, if only they could be allowed to get back to England where they had already got homes and even wives. They were not informed of what was happening, did not know what was being done about their case, and were just living from day to day in an atmosphere of terror and uncertainty. I listened with growing indignation. I could feel for them in their predicament. Like cattle they were being shunted around, waiting for the slaughter, and as I later met some of the

crew and their women folk who had travelled with them, I realised how simple and trusting these people were.

I asked him if they had ever made an official protest. They had
not. English was a foreign language to them, although they all
spoke it in a broken fashion. He looked so pleadingly at me when
he asked if I could help in any way, that I gave the matter some
thought. I said that at least their plight should be put down in black
and white and handed to the Ministry of Transport representative
of the Mission. I decided I would write a petition for them which
all could sign, simply stating they had been in the past faithful servants of His Majesty's Government, wanted to continue being so,
their situation at present was such and such and they wanted
nothing more than to be shipped back to England by any means
possible. I carefully translated this to the whole of the crew whom I
met later. They signed it, as though it was a passport to Heaven.
Poor devils. It at least gave them some sort of hope. I never found
out what eventually happened to them. I know their Captain
handed it in for them and the copies I made for them, which they
also signed, were regarded as treasured possessions among themselves.

I knew it had been handed in because I received a severe reprimand with an injunction not to meddle in affairs that did not concern me. This came through my Chief. It was official, but it was
kind of half-hearted, because when I related their story to my Chief,
he understood the situation.

The weeks had gone by like lightning, Group Captain Bird
could not hang on to me any longer, orders were orders. The next
homeward bound convoy was leaving on 25 November, 1941.
The ship I was to sail on was the *Temple Arch* which was docked at
Molotovsk, a port some eight to ten miles from Archangel. This
news made me very downhearted for Nora was never far from my
mind. On the night of the 12th November, as I went wearily to my
room, the old Russian war-horse guarding the corridor relaxed her
features to give me the faintest suspicion of a smile. I was really
taken aback for she was always so grim-visaged, and when
Russians smile their whole features change. There is nothing so
warm as a Russian smile. Maybe it's the climate that does it. It set
me thinking. There was a telephone hanging on the wall in the

corridor. I often wondered whether it was in working order. I decided one night to ask the porteress if she could get me Moscow on the line, and gave her my house number. I explained I had a little Russian *devushka* (girl) with whom I was deeply in love and as I was soon to leave Archangel, I wanted to say good-bye. I told her this and looked terribly sad, for I felt sad. Her face lit up into a full smile. Certainly she would try for me she said. What an awful thing to happen to anybody!

She took the phone and said something to the exchange operator and then I heard her repeat my telephone number. There was a short pause, then she thrust the receiver into my hands and said, '*Vot!*' Clear and distinct, Nora's voice came over the 'phone, '*Kto tam?*' (Who's there?')

'Nora!' I said. 'It's John.' I almost felt her swaying.

'Oh, John. Where are you?'

'I'm here, in Archangel, speaking from the Intourist. I have received orders to leave for England. I am leaving in twelve days' time, but I'll come back for you, Nora. Wait for me. I promise I'll come back for you.'

'John, John, I love you so. I'll come to Archangel,' she gasped.

I was alarmed. 'Don't try, Nora. It's dangerous. Everywhere the lines are under fire.'

'I'm coming———!'

The line suddenly went dead. I handed the receiver back to the porteress. She rattled it and spoke a few words into the mouthpiece then turned to me and said, 'The line's been cut,' shaking her head mournfully. I was surprised that we had got through at all. It seemed a miracle to me, especially as I knew the railway from Moscow to Archangel had been repeatedly cut by enemy action near Vologda.

Actually, I never gave another thought to the possibility of Nora carrying out her intention to come. First, once she left the house she would be picked up by the Police. Secondly, the only method of travel was by train and the line was insecure owing to the German advance, and thirdly, only such persons as were permitted by the NKVD were allowed to board the trains, which were constantly searched and checked throughout every journey. At this time, only military personnel were using them and they, of course, could not run to a definite schedule.

I tried many times to get through to Moscow again, but all to no avail. My hours of duty were still long and arduous. We were so terribly short staffed and there were still constant bickerings with the Russians who interfered with our men on the unloading of the armaments for Russia. All this led to a lot of unnecessary friction and suspicion. The only members of the Mission who achieved any sort of friendly relationship were our Naval personnel, some of whom were even allowed to sail on their ships. The biggest shock our naval officers got on such trips was the Soviet employment of women naval officers – captains, engineers, the lot! It took ages for the Senior Service to get over the shock of women's encroachment into a man's world. A bigger shock still was their efficiency. Alas, our people knew so very little of the real Russia!

At last the dreaded day when I was to leave Russia arrived. On 25 November, 1941, I boarded *Temple Arch*, but not without first a close scrutiny and thorough search of my belongings by the Russian Police and frontier controllers. I felt utterly weary and dispirited and must have looked it because the Captain invited me to have a drink with him. I told him the cause of my despondency was a Russian girl I'd had to leave behind and that she was in danger and I did not know what to do. Of course I could not tell him the whole story, but he was very sympathetic and tried to cheer me up. Some of the crew were on the quayside having a game of football, a final opportunity to stretch their legs on terra firma for we were due to sail at dawn. I went on deck and leant on the rail to watch them. It was about three p.m. Six powerful overhead lamps lit up the scene. Dusk was already approaching. The lamps, by the way, were to enable the Russians to keep the ship under observation until it left. Already the ground was covered with a thick carpet of snow and it was still falling, but our lads were thoroughly enjoying their game. I'd been watching them for a few minutes when in the distance I noticed a figure weaving and stumbling in the snow, approaching our ship. At first I thought it was some poor devil who had escaped the chain-gang. Not an infrequent event, sometimes a prisoner did break loose, the sight of a slop basin being emptied from a ship's side being too much for the half-starved creatures. Men had been known to scramble to a ship to gather up the waste food that was emptied overboard. They were generally clubbed before they could achieve their purpose. As the figure approached nearer, the whole universe seemed to sway round me. I could hardly believe my eyes. It was Nora! She had seen me and was crying, 'John, John!' I was over that deck in a flash and fairly leapt down the gangway, nearly knocking the Russian guard over as I sprinted to meet Nora. How can I describe that moment when we fell into each other's arms; even I cried from the shock. I could hardly believe it was real.

Ignoring the menacing action of the guard with an '*Idi k chortn*' (Go to the devil!) I led her up the gangway into the ship. There was pandemonium as the game of football stopped and the crew came up and stood around us – all I could say was 'Nora, Nora,' over and again. The Captain came up and shepherded us into his cabin and ordered the steward to bring tea instantly. Nora was half-frozen and shaking like a leaf. I turned to the Captain and said, 'This is Nora – the girl I have been telling you about. How she's got here, God only knows.'

The Captain finally soothed us both down into a semblance of sanity and we began to take stock of the situation. I'd already made up my mind what was to be done. We were on a British ship, the Captain could marry us and we'd sail for England together. I saw no obstacles in the way. But the Captain, poor fellow, suffered with us as he pointed out that we were still in Russia and he had no power to do what I begged. He would not only have to get permission from the Russians but our own authorities. As we were going over this problem the door burst open and in strode a couple of NKVD officers. Their commands were peremptory. Nora must leave the ship instantly. She was an unauthorised person. I asked Nora if she had any documents on her. She had! It was a most imposing official-looking document indeed. It was a foolscap sheet, headed with the emblem of the United States Embassy to which was attached a magnificent beribboned seal with the American Eagle. Her photograph was also stamped on it, and it enjoined all aid to be given to Citizeness, Nora Nina Korzhenko, in carrying out her duties to deliver the personal effects of British Embassy official, John Murray, to Archangel.

The officers were quite awed by this but stuck to their orders that she must leave the ship and this forbidden territory and go back to Archangel and they would personally see her safely there. We could do nothing. There was a very tearful farewell and we parted once again. I was at my wits' end, bitter, disappointed, and still feeling the effects of the shock of our meeting – everything seemed unreal, I thought it was a dream. I was for leaving the ship immediately and going back to Archangel, but the Captain said my official embarkation orders were still with him and it would be more than his life was worth to allow me to disobey them. He pointed to a small hut on the quayside.

'There's a telephone connected to the Mission in there, ring them up for instructions.'

I did so and was lucky to be able to get Group Captain Bird first time. I quickly explained my position. 'Stay where you are, Murray. I'll send someone over right away to bring you off!' He could have said otherwise, but he was now repaying me for all I'd done for him. I felt grateful.

Within an hour Sasha Fisher drove up in a car and handed me a document officially recalling me from the ship. Saying farewell and wishing the Captain and crew a speedy and safe voyage I drove away with Sasha to our headquarters at Norwegian House. When I arrived there, Group Captain Bird, after listening to my profuse thanks, gave me an odd quizzical smile.

'Well, John, what are you going to do now? I can't keep you here for ever.' I told him that to me Nora was more than my housekeeper. I had fallen in love with her long ago, and it had been and was my intention to marry her and get her out of the country at the first available opportunity.

'Well, the best of luck, John. You've certainly got a job on your hands.'

He was of course glad of the excuse to have me back, but there was still something I could not understand.

Sasha drove me back to the Intourist Hotel. On the way he explained that he had met Nora when she had arrived, and had put her in my room. He had known who she was from what I had told him of her. He had reported her arrival the day before to Group Captain Bird as she had brought along with her from Moscow a whole cartload of my effects. The Group Captain had told him to tell her I had already embarked on my ship for home, the news had shattered her.

When we arrived, I dashed straight up to my room. Nora lay on the bed sobbing. For some minutes she could hardly realise it was I who had come, and kept touching me to see if I was real. I told her my Chief had recalled me at the last moment, just before sailing. Again it would be hard even to attempt to describe the joy at our reunion. We spent practically the whole of that night talking, questioning and counter-questioning. Bit by bit I got the whole story out of her.

She explained that Sir Noel Mason MacFarlane and Air Vice-Marshal Collier had returned to Moscow from Kuibyshev and following some vicious air attacks on Moscow the two of them had decided to make a spot check upon my former place in *Maly kharitonevsky* to see if everything was all right. Probably they had also received a hint from Dunlop, the Embassy Secretary, that my housekeeper was an undesirable (from the Russian point of view).

Now MacFarlane, though a rough and ready soldier of stern appearance, was in fact a very warm-hearted man, and Nora, sensing this had told them the whole story of our relationship and her past. It must have been a shock to both he and the Air Vice-Marshal, but the pathos of her story must have touched him deeply and he assured her of his protection. Collier, however, was furious and when he later arrived in Kuibyshev issued the command for me to be sent home under the guise of ill health, without giving me any explanations of what had transpired. By that merest chance of getting through to Nora by 'phone from Archangel, a whole sequence of events followed. Nora, frantic and out of her mind, remembered my instructions as to what to do in an emergency and decided to contact Reinhardt at the American Embassy. Reinhardt did not hesitate to help her. Nora's only desire was to get to Archangel, no matter what the cost, to see me if only for once more. It drove her on to achieve the impossible. Reinhardt supplied her with an American protective pass that even the Russians dared not ignore. He also gave her the necessary money and even had the Embassy car drive her to the station, all official and business-like. It was only her supreme courage and audacity, spurred on by love, that carried her through in those dark and dangerous days.

When she had arrived at the Intourist Hotel in Archangel, she met Sasha Fisher who told her I was already aboard the *Temple Arch*. She was heart-broken as well as exhausted. Later, driven by hunger, she was compelled to go down to the restaurant for some food. Imagine the mutual shock and surprise when she came face to face with Gabaridze. He already knew my story and was kind to Nora. Whether accidentally or on purpose, he sat her at the table occupied by my friend the Esthonian Captain. The kindly old Captain, watching her eat with tears falling down her face all the time, asked her what was wrong. Nora, now realising all was lost and not caring what might happen, poured out the whole story to him. He understood the situation immediately. He let her finish and said, 'Why, you must be John's Nora. He told me all about you! He has not gone yet. His ship is due to leave the day after tomorrow. He is still in Russia!' He then gave her minute details of how to get to my ship. How, that it lay in a strictly forbidden area and special permits would be needed for all the Security Stations guarding the way. He told her what to avoid and all the snags, and finally warned her how dangerous it would be. They decided that it would be best for her to attempt to reach my ship in the morning. She succeeded, thanks to this brave old seaman.

I now looked around our room. There were two large suitcases and fifteen bundles of various sizes. Bundles wrapped in sheets and blankets, carefully sewn up. It was staggering. These were some of my effects that Nora had packed and brought with her. I could not imagine how she had managed to bring so much. Nora told me that Rebecca had helped her to gather and sew up the bundles. There were clothes, tinned conserves and most extraordinary of all, my glassware consisting of brandy, wine, liqueur, hock and champagne glasses that I'd used for entertaining. Some three hundred pieces in all, carefully wrapped in toilet paper. To me, they were of little value. I had bought them off Bagshawe before he left. They looked beautiful but in fact were all Woolworth's stuff that he'd had sent over from England years ago. The average price had been half-a-crown a set of one dozen. She'd managed to see that not one had been broken on the journey. Even today I still marvel how she was able to bring this stuff at such a time.

As we went on talking we came to the inevitable question of

what to do next. I was determined not to lose her again and was still frightened of the long arm of the NKVD. One thing I was determined on, by hook or by crook we would get married. To Nora the idea still seemed an impossibility, but we agreed that the next day we would make enquiries as to how this could be done. It was already the early hours of a new day. We slept in each other's arms, once again confident we would be able to win through and the little Madonna that Nora unpacked seemed to shed peace on our slumbers. The morning came all too soon, but we were buoyed up by our excitement. The first thing I did was to telephone the Group Captain for time off to attend to my affairs (meaning Nora). He gave me a free hand. Next, I introduced Nora to our 'watchdog' – the lady who sat on the chair that commanded a view of the corridor on that floor. We told her we wanted to get married and asked her how we should go about it. She actually beamed – this was a unique romance for her hotel. She explained that we should go to the Marriage Bureau Registry at the municipal building, gave us directions, and wished us well.

Breakfast over, supervised by Gabaridze to whom we mentioned our project and to which he, too, wished us well, we set out. The marriage registrar, who was a woman, was quite astounded at our request. Nothing like this had ever happened before in Archangel. She would love to marry us she said, but she did not know what regulation applied to a Soviet citizeness marrying a foreigner and advised us to see the Chief of Police for the Archangel District, giving us instructions of where to go. So off we marched to the Chief of Police, a Major Dritz. He, too, was astounded, but told us he could not do anything himself because it was a matter for the Chief of the NKVD. He would give us the necessary permit and recommendation to go to the NKVD building where we were to ask for Major Sokolov who was responsible for the security for all Archangel.

We went to him after being passed from one guard to another. He was very abrupt and guarded when we explained our intentions and begged his help. He told us he could not give an answer, but we were to call back in two days' time. I knew then that it was a case of his getting instructions from Moscow, and I determined there and then that the only weapon we had, was to spread around to every Russian official person with whom I had contact, and my job entailed many such contacts, that Nora and I were truly in love and would surely get the blessing of the Soviet authorities seeing that I was working so hard in the Military Mission bringing aid to Russia. All this, of course, would be reported to the 'right quarters' and open them up to public censorship should they refuse our request. In a way it worked: all Archangel seemed to be buzzing with the gossip of this most extraordinary romance. Quite a number of people came into the Intourist restaurant, just to look at us during meal times and would greet us with sympathetic nods.

Meanwhile, unbeknown to me at the time, Group Captain Bird had reported my situation direct to Sir Noel Mason MacFarlane and he had contacted Sir Stafford Cripps and they were both subsequently to plead my case personally with Stalin himself several times, much to Stalin's annoyance over such a triviality while the war was on. They were rebuffed each time as I later found out. When we went to Sokolov we were further put off and more brusquely than ever. I was frightened and forbade Nora ever to leave our hotel room whilst I was away on duty. Sometimes I took her to work with me to the Military Mission's mess room to wait for me, but this was later forbidden. This added to my anxieties. Nora received a summons some days after to call at the NKVD office alone, but I accompanied her and after a bit of a row was allowed in with her to see Major Sokolov. He told us that the Moscow authorities had demanded that Nora return immediately to Moscow as she had no legal Russian documents. If she went she would be granted them and probably would afterwards be permitted to marry me. It all seemed so vague and I demanded that the documents be sent to Archangel instead. He began to get really nasty and said those were the instructions and if she did not carry them out she would be arrested on the spot and be dealt with accordingly. Once again I felt that terrible fear for Nora's safety.

Nora came back with me to the hotel. I gave Group Captain Bird an account of our interview. He said nothing but called in Sasha and they went to see Major Sokolov to sort things out on my behalf. They returned some two hours later but gave me no account of what had transpired at their meeting, except gravely to inform me that it definitely would be necessary for Nora to leave for Moscow, Sokolov assuring them that Nora would not be molested in any way and she would get her necessary documents. Nora and I talked it over with my chief. There was nothing we could do. I was depressed, and suggested that I be allowed to travel with her. My chief said no, as I was still under embarkation orders, but he then informed me that he had been in touch with Sir Noel who had informed him that both Sir Stafford Cripps and himself were again speaking with Stalin about us. This was good news to us, and we agreed that Nora should leave.

Sasha and I saw Nora on to the train. It was another sad and tearful parting full of mingled fears and hopes.

Over a week went by and still no news from Nora came through. We had arranged that on her arrival in Moscow she would let me know of her safe arrival via the Embassy. I managed to get calls through the Mission 'phone both to the Embassy and Rebecca at *Maly kharitonevsky* to ask if she had arrived. That answer was that they had neither seen nor heard from her. In spite of Sokolov's guards I made my way to him and threatened that I'd shoot him if I found out that anything had happened to Nora; I was in such a frantic rage. He protested that everything would be all right. I got home and gradually cooled down and began to think what I could do next. The man who was the cause of the trouble was the head of the NKVD, Beria. I decided to send him a cable and compiled a long telegram in Russian, stating who I was and the fact that I was helping the Soviets by my service with the British Mission that was bringing aid to Russia and all I begged of him was to use his power to allow me to marry the Russian girl I loved, and I would be deeply grateful for all the help he could give me.

It was a very long telegram and the woman in the Post Office looked shocked when I handed it in. I asked her if it would reach Beria; she said certainly as no one would care to intercept a telegram addressed to him personally. Within seven days we got the message through from the Embassy that Nora had reported to them. She had been granted her documents and was on her way back to Archangel and the question of permission to marry would be decided by the NKVD in Archangel.

This was the most heartening news I could ever have received and I counted every minute until her arrival. As the trains from

Moscow ran indeterminately, sometimes once every five days or ten days dependent on the fighting in the area, I kept a check on the railway activity and was able, with Sasha, to be at the station when the train bringing her arrived on 20 January, 1942. What can I say about the happiness of our reunion – no words of mine can do justice to the joy and happiness we felt. We got back to the Intourist Hotel and there was all the excitement of our own people and even the Russian staff of the hotel and others who were amazed at Nora's return. Everyone had thought that I would never see her again. Nora gave me an account of what had happened after the train had steamed out of Archangel.

The first three days of the journey had been uneventful. At midnight on the fourth day, two armed NKVD officers had entered her compartment and ordered her to pack her things and be ready to leave the train at the next stop. What station it was, she did not know. She was escorted off and marched to a building, put in an empty room and her escort left her there without any explanation, locking the door behind them as they left. She was terrified, not knowing what was going to happen. She was kept there for four days and nights, but was given food and only allowed out to the adjacent toilet room. No word was spoken to her and whenever she attempted to speak was sternly ordered to shut up. She could hear no movement of trains or vehicles. There was nothing but silence. The fourth day a train steamed into the station. The door of her room was opened and an officer walked in and told her to get her things and board the train which would take her to Moscow. She arrived without any incident and went straight to *Maly kharitonevsky*.

From there she telephoned Sir Noel who came to see her and told her to have courage as he was doing all he could for her. She later reported to the District Police Officer as she had been instructed to do by Major Sokolov before she left Archangel. With some trepidation, not knowing what would happen, she once again entered the Police Headquarters from where I had rescued her during that memorable night of the air raids. She was surprised at the reception she got. Although not cordial it was not altogether unfriendly. She was given a new set of Russian identity documents, passport, and informed that she was now a free citizeness of the

Soviet Union and should be thankful her civil rights had been restored to her. After reporting to Sir Noel she once again was escorted and put on the train for Archangel. It almost seemed like a dream.

We got another surprise of tremendous importance two days later. At the ungodly hour of midnight we were summoned by a police officer to accompany him to the Chief of Police Office to see Major Dritz. With our hearts in our mouths, not knowing what was to happen next, we came face to face. He greeted us with a smile and apologised for bringing us in so late, but he had good news for us and was sure that we'd agree he had done the right thing. Instructions had just been received that our permit to get married had been granted! After all we had gone through it seemed as though miracles were happening. We embraced one another and danced round Major Dritz's room like a couple of demented persons and the Major just sat at his desk and laughed. 'Now,' he broke in, 'when *do* you want to get married?' If the marriage office had been open we'd have flown there right away. 'Can we get married in the morning?' we asked. 'Certainly! Now go – I've a lot of work to do!' We shook hands and returned to our hotel as if in a dream. What a night!

The morning seemed as if it would never come, but when it did Nora rushed round telling everybody we were going to get married, and I got on the phone to Group Captain Bird and told him the news. He was full of congratulations. The Intourist was in an uproar. The Russians could hardly believe it. The first to congratulate us was Gabaridze who said he'd make a wedding party that very night for us and all our guests. All he could do was to shake his massive head repeating '*Vot, vot, vot!*' Nora and I went to the Zags Bureau, the State Registry Office for Marriages, at its ten o'clock opening time. We were ushered into a medium-sized room with just a desk at which was seated the marriage official, a woman, whom I would say was in her forties. Very pleasing and very businesslike. On both sides of the desk stood two pedestals, one adorned with the bust of Karl Marx and the other with the bust of Lenin. A huge picture of Stalin imposed on the Red Flag adorned the background. I left all the talking to Nora. We were both handed a much-thumbed card on which was a list of various diseases starting with tuberculosis, insanity, venereal disease. We had to affirm that neither we nor our families suffered from any of these.

Then the marriage code was read out to us, the gist of which was that we would be faithful and helpful to one another at all times and be good and lawful citizens. Then Nora was asked what name she would adopt for her marriage – her husband's or still retain her own. At once Nora said mine. But it was pointed out that it was quite unusual now to adopt the husband's name and she was quite free to keep her own name. But Nora insisted on her decision.

Then a Register was handed over to us to sign. A clerk, who was also a woman but much younger, came in, took the Register into another office where a marriage certificate was prepared, and brought it back for the marriage official to stamp and sign. Even our passports were asked for as they too had to be stamped with the record of our marriage. We were then handed the duly completed marriage certificate, shaken by the hand in turn and pronounced as lawful man and wife.

We went out in a daze. Everything seemed to be happening.

Gabaridze's party for us that night was a thing to remember. I invited as many members of the Mission as I could – the Navy, Air Force and Army were all well represented and from the Russian side quite a number of NKVD officers including one of the Governors and his wife, in charge of one of the prison camps. They were frequenters of the Intourist whom I had met before. This Governor had been a high-ranking NKVD officer in Moscow, but as a sign of displeasure had been demoted to this job in Archangel. As the Intourist was the only social centre in this God-forsaken part of Russia, he and his wife found relief in coming to it from the inhumane and distasteful, as well as dangerous job he had been forced to take. It is not my intention to relate the many stories he told me concerning the actions he was unwillingly forced to take in the execution of his duties. Even the most broad-minded would not believe them.

Gabaridze even produced Russian Champagne for the unending round of toasts that were drunk. The orchestra played for us incessantly. Our old Esthonian sea captain with many of his crew, including the women, were there. The party was a huge success.

There was an atmosphere of friendliness and goodwill all round and I was subjected to much leg-pulling and good-humoured marital advice. Everyone seemed glad of the opportunity to forget their fears and sorrows for at least one evening, and this applied to the Russians too. We had plenty to drink in the way of Vodka. Our Mission lads, unaccustomed to the potency of it, drank a lot without feeling its effects in the warm and crowded restaurant. It was only when they got out into the open cold air that its full effects became evident. They would be walking back when suddenly, after staggering along for a bit, they would keel over and flop into the mounds of snow on the side-walks, and a busy time was had by organising search parties to dig them out before they froze.

All in all it was a happy and enjoyable party, but I could not help feeling a tinge of guilt about being so happy, when all around us there was such an element of deepest misery and despair. My marriage was reported to our Embassy in Moscow and diplomatic action was put in motion to effect Nora's departure with me as my lawful wife. Two weeks later, Group Captain Bird called me into his office for a personal talk. His face had a very serious look. He told me that the Embassy's request had been rejected out of hand. I would be allowed to leave Russia any time, but Nora could only leave when the war was over, as in spite of our marriage she was, by Soviet Law, still a Russian subject and as such could not claim British Nationality whilst on Russian soil and as there was no agreement in existence between our two countries that could deal with the case, there was absolutely nothing that could be done.

The only solution to this problem would be a decree to be passed by the Supreme Soviet giving Soviet subjects the right to renounce their nationality if they could first prove that the country of their adoption would accept them. Such a decree was not in existence. As all this depended upon such a decree being passed by the Supreme Soviet, it was pointed out that such trivia could not even be entertained by the Soviet Government who had more urgent priorities to consider.

When I heard this my heart sank. The Group Captain then went on to say that in view of this state of affairs, for security reasons laid down by the Foreign Office I would either have to leave the

country, in which case I would be transferred to the British Legation in Istanbul, or, I would have to face dismissal from the service.
As I realised the full portent of what he said, I felt really depressed.
Up to this time, my hopes had been buoyed by the permission we
had received to get married. This news however was a bombshell!
But I was determined. I would not leave Archangel without my
wife, and I told him so. He asked me to think it over very carefully
and let him know the next day. When I arrived at the hotel I told
Nora the news. She looked at me dumbly. I could read the anguish
in her face. I clasped her tightly, 'Don't worry, Nora. I'll never
leave you!' The following day, 5 February, 1942, I told Group
Captain Bird of my decision.

I typed out my own Notice of Termination of Employment at
his dictation, which he signed. It read:

'You are hereby notified that your appointment as clerk to the
Attaché, Moscow, will terminate one month from today's date.' It
was dated 5 February, 1942. I carried on with my duties throughout the month of my notice, and as there was so much to be done, I
was heavily occupied.

As my term of notice drew to an end, I began to give some
thought to the serious position Nora and I were in. One thing, my
rouble allowance would stop and I would need roubles for us both
if we were staying on in Archangel indefinitely. For one English
pound which I could only exchange officially through a Russian
Bank, I would get three-and-a-half roubles. I had already
enquired the cost of staying in the Intourist, the only hotel in
Archangel, and the price was seventy-five roubles per day for full
board for each of us! As far as I knew, I had only a matter of
£1500 in the bank in England. I never was any good at figures,
but even I realised that our position was bordering on disaster, and
I did not want to add to Nora's worries if I could help it. Turning
things over in my mind, I realised that in a country like Russia
everything, including one's existence depended upon one man,
and one man alone – Stalin, and that was the only course left open
to us – to appeal to him direct. I discussed with Nora, who being
Russian, understood what I was getting at. Eventually we decided
on sending him two telegrams, one from her and one from myself.
To my question, would he receive it, she assured me that, as in the

case of the telegrams I had sent to Beria, no one would dare inter-
rupt or interfere with a communication addressed personally to
Stalin, not even Beria. That it would be handed to him, she knew
that for sure. We set about composing the two telegrams. That
from Nora read:

> 'Gospodin Stalin. I am a loyal Russian Subject and have mar-
> ried John Murray of the British Embassy whom I love very
> dearly. I plead with you Gospodin Stalin to allow me to travel
> to England with him as he is being sent back to his country.'

The one from me read:

> 'Gospodin Stalin. I have done all I can to help Russia. You,
> Gospodin Stalin, are the only person in the whole wide world
> that can help me now for I must return to my own country
> and I wish to take my Russian wife whom I truly love with
> me. I beg your help to enable me to do this, Gospodin Stalin.'

Nora made the telegrams out in her bold Russian handwriting
and we set off, hand in hand, to the Archangel Post Office. The
woman counter-hand's face was a picture as she counted the large
number of words and digested the contents of the telegrams.
Those telegrams I knew would pass through many hands before
they reached Stalin, but receive them he would. A load seemed
to be lifted off our minds as we returned home. There was
nothing more we could do but hope.

The telegrams were sent off on 1 March, 1942. If Stalin really
wanted to do anything, I knew our dossiers would be called for
from the NKVD. Apart from Nora's espionage career, there was
nothing that could be held against us. I, in particular, had been
careful to maintain a friendly personal attitude towards all the
Russians I had met knowing full well all would be recorded
somewhere or other. My term of office ultimately came to an
end, although I did not carry on with the confidential stuff, in
order to comply with the security code, I gave a hand wherever
possible in the Mission and in order to save on the bit of money I
possessed, had my meals in the Mission mess, a kind of unwritten

arrangement accepted by all.

Nora throughout this period was kept quite busy which was as well for me, as it was imperative she should have something to take her mind off our precarious predicament. Her demeanour by now had undergone a complete change, she was smiling, cheerful, with a friendly word for everyone. She was well liked. Gone once more was that fear and hunted expression from her features.

Into the Intourist Hotel batches of Poles had begun to arrive. They were quartered in tens to twenty persons per room and the hotel was full of them. In charge were two Polish ex-officers – Pan Gruya and Pan Loga. The Poles were coming in from various labour camps throughout the Siberian and Archangel areas. They were being freed to join the Polish forces. There were women among them as well as men. Their condition was pitiful. A train was being organised by the Russians to take them on their long journey to Persia from whence they would be shipped to England. The two Pans' work was enormous. The Russians were only grudgingly setting the Poles free. From their point of view they were only useless cattle. Nora worked with them to prepare their bits of belongings and advise on the necessities for the long journey that lay before them. All this kept her busy and I was thankful for it.

When 'the shoe began to pinch' moneywise, I was able to sell my stainless steel wrist-watch that I'd brought from Sweden (bought there for £35) to one of the Russian officers who'd long admired it and could never take his eyes off it when we met. When I offered to sell it to him, he was tremendously grateful. Few Russians had watches at that time and those Russians who had looked ridiculous – their watches were like big alarm clocks strapped to their wrists. We did not even discuss price. He just took the watch off me and handled it as though it were some precious jewel. Then he put his hand into his tunic pocket and brought out a fistful of rouble notes that I pocketed without even counting. When I showed them to Nora there were three thousand roubles in that handful! Following this, Nora, who had become friendly with the wife of the Commandant of the Archangel labour camp sold my glassware to her for five thousand roubles! She had often seen them and admired them whenever she came, ever curious, to our room for a chat with Nora and I was quite willing for her to have them. Nora found that she could dispose of other oddments, too, especially some of the clothes I had which were of no use to me. Poor girl, she herself had no clothes of her own beyond one dress and a set of underwear – because in those days clothes were not available; even if I gave her money she would not have been able to buy any. She wore my underwear of which I had a fair stock and one of my tweed suits and seemed quite content.

There was one other thing that happened. When Nora and I finally got permission for our marriage, she had sent a telegram to Tashkent, to the last address she had heard from her exiled stepmother, who had now been joined by her step-grandmother and little Felix her stepbrother. Nora received a short reply saying a letter to us was on the way – about three weeks later the letter arrived. In it her stepmother said they were as well as could be expected. She had been able to find work helping on a farm, but her mother was ailing and little Felix was weak through lack of proper food, and if Nora could only send a few hundred roubles to her, she could purchase a goat to obtain milk for the boy. Nora and I decided that we would send what we could from our meagre store and eventually sent two lots of money by telegraph. One was for five hundred and the other for one thousand roubles. As the Polish repatriation train would be passing near Tashkent, Nora began to sew up a couple of parcels with what was left of our tinned goods from Moscow and clothes from my wardrobe and also a primus-cooker that I had managed to obtain. The Polish people promised they would see that her stepmother got them. She never did. Why, I do not know.

Just about the middle of April, Gabaridze came to our room, his face twitching – he looked to be in great distress. As we invited him to sit, he broke down and cried. He had just received a notification that his only son had been killed at the front. Nora and I wept with him. His anguish was terrible. There are situations when one feels really helpless. I went downstairs to get a drink for the want of something better to do. Gabaridze I left, his head on Nora's breast weeping, while she stroked his thin greying hair, murmuring her sympathy in Russian. When I returned some time later he had gone. From that day the light left his eyes and he carried on with his duties like an automaton, there was only a twitchy grimace left on his face to replace the warm soft smile he used to have.

On 17 April, 1942, in the early hours of the morning (it was two a.m.) there was a loud knock on our door. When we opened it, an NKVD officer stood outside.

'Citizeness Korzhenko, you are to come with me to Headquarters, Major Sokolov will speak to you!'

Terrified, we both got up and though the officer insisted that only Nora went, I accompanied them. We arrived at Major Sokolov's headquarters and Nora was conducted to his room. I had to stay outside. A great fear welled up inside me. I waited for what seemed ages. Then I saw Nora being escorted from the corridor. She walked as if in a dream and her face had a stunned look.

'Let us go home,' she said.

I knew something of very great importance must have transpired, but she seemed to be in such a pitch of suppressed excitement, I thought it best not to question her but let her tell me in her own good time. The thing that mattered to me at the moment was that she'd come out safe and sound, and my relief at that was enough. When we got back to our room, she suddenly hugged me and cried, 'I'm free!' She then went on to tell me what had happened.

When she was conducted to Major Sokolov's room, there was another officer standing beside his desk. He introduced her to him and explained that this officer had just arrived from Moscow on a special mission from Comrade Stalin. The Supreme Soviet had passed a special decree whereby, providing the country of her husband would officially accept her into their country as the lawful wedded wife of her husband, she would be permitted under this decree to renounce her Soviet citizenship and leave Russia. If this was her final wish, she was to report to Major Dritz, the Chief of the Police, who would arrange the necessary documents for her to sign and issue her with a visa to leave the country. When she had finished, I could well understand the reason for her looking so stunned.

I contacted Group Captain Bird at the first opportunity to tell him the news and he called us to his office.

After congratulating us, he went to his desk, unlocked one of the drawers, took out a British Passport and gave it to Nora. She looked at it with a kind of holy awe, kissed it, and suddenly flung her arms round the startled Captain and kissed him too, tears of happiness running down her cheeks all the while. We then went on to Major Dritz at the Police Headquarters. Again I was not allowed at the interview, but the Major finally came out with Nora and, shaking my hands, wished me the best of luck and every happiness. Nora explained later what had happened. She was told Stalin himself had given personal consideration to her case. The document for renunciation of her Soviet citizenship was there for her to sign providing her husband's country accepted her. She signed the paper after handing her British Passport over to him. It was stamped and signed with an exit visa valid for three months. She was told that the authorities were sorry for the difficulties she had experienced, but they had only been carrying out their duties. She was never to forget that she was a Russian, and not to bring disgrace to the country of her birth.

After this, events began to move rapidly and Group Captain Bird informed me that the Mission were preparing an outward-bound convoy and Nora and I would shortly receive embarkation papers to board one of the ships that would be sailing in it. Later I went down to Molotovsk to have a look and watch the giant Russian icebreaker, *Stalin*, crashing through the thick ice that carpeted the White Sea in order to make a lane for the ships to pass through. This was a remarkable sight. The *Stalin* was a huge black ship, broad of beam, with an unusually blunt bow. It would move slowly forward and then come crashing down on the ice beneath. This would break and shatter the ice with a sound like big guns booming, to the accompaniment of loud sharp cracking noises. Backwards and forwards it would move all the time until long black streaks of water could be seen. The ship chosen for us was the SS *Empire Stevenson*, we were to board her as soon as she was ready – approximately some two days before the convoy was due to start. As Group Captain Bird said, 'Better get aboard before the Russians change their minds.'

Part VI

The Convoys of Death

By this time both Nora and I were in a state of physical and mental exhaustion. Every knock at our door had made us jump, and knowing how things could change without cause or explanation, we were both tense with the uncertainty of our situation – things seemed too good to last.

We boarded the SS *Empire Stevenson* on 21 April, 1942. For security purposes Nora was signed on in the official ship's log book as 'stewardess' and I as 'assistant steward' and we were given the steward's cabin which, though small, was quite comfortable.

As soon as we embarked we were followed by the Russian passport and customs control officers to examine our, by now, very meagre possessions. The former did their duty of stamping our passports quickly and silently. In my baggage I had about thirty figurines carved from mammoth bones dug up in the Siberian wastes and fashioned by prisoners in the labour camps. They were beautiful and delicate works of art – reindeer, hunters, and various animals. I had been able to procure them in return for tins of conserves from various needy looking individuals that one would occasionally see standing about the streets of Archangel, just dumbly offering their figurines from upturned hands. The big burly customs man, looking twice as big in a shaggy sheepskin coat, called me into our cabin. 'Uh! What are these?' he said. All I could think of to say whilst shrugging my shoulders was, 'Presents.' Without a word he crushed them in his hands. I could say or do nothing, except silently wish that one day his turn would come. Knowing Russia, it probably did.

We spent the next two days getting acquainted with the crew and the ship, which was a six-thousand ton merchant ship. She was loaded with timber. Even the upper decks were stacked with it. From then on, until we sailed, we were not allowed to go off the ship. The steward's cabin was situated near the stern of the ship, just behind the twelve-pounder. The adjoining cabin had been converted into a powder magazine for the gun and the rear wall of our cabin stacked with depth charges.

The date of sailing arrived – 27 April, 1942. In the distance the other ships from various quaysides in the White Sea began to converge to take sailing orders. It was a bit cramped in the beginning as there was only a limited area of water freed from the ice. Slowly we steamed out as our turn came. We were the last in the line. No waving friends to see us off. Only the silent figures of the Russian port guards could be seen against the grim receding coastline. The first day of the journey was uncanny. We were actually on our way to England. Everything seemed like a dream. We could not talk in anything but awed whispers to each other.

The convoy we sailed in was the QP 10 and consisted of sixteen ships. We were due to cross with the convoy PQ14* from England at a point in the Arctic Circle near Bear Island. The convoy consisted of twenty-four ships which were bringing arms and munitions to Russia.

When the two convoys did meet they were attacked by German destroyers, submarines and aircraft, and four of our ships in the convoy were sent to the bottom. But our ship was not among them. It happened like this.

Our ship had been steaming along following the others for about four hours when there was a heavy jolt, and the whole ship began to shake from the vibration of the propeller shaft revolving at a tremendous speed as though the engines had suddenly gone wild. The engines were cut off as we all rushed to the side of the ship and men came tumbling up from the hatches. It was soon ascertained that our propeller had been broken. By some mischance the propeller had fouled a submerged block of ice. The ice in those parts was of quite unbelievable toughness. When you consider the winter temperature is an unending ten to twenty and more degrees below zero, day in and day out, without any let-up

* The PQ convoys were those sailing to Russia.
The QP convoys were those returning home from Russia.

for nearly six months on end, it is no wonder that it was so. The sea anchors were dropped and we remained stationary, the rest of our convoy sailed on without us. More than four weeks were to elapse before we could move again.

After a couple of days we were boarded by Royal Naval divers who were to check the damage. It was confirmed that the blades of the screw had been broken off and we heard that a new screw was to be flown over from England. As the weeks went by, one could feel a mounting tension all round. The crew were kept busy round the clock, working in shifts. Lowered overboard with poles and stanchions they would push the ice-floes away from the ship to prevent us getting iced in. A constant watch had to be kept on this ice. Meanwhile I was co-opted for gunnery practice. We would spend hours training on the twelve-pounder which was mounted on the stern of the ship. This took some of the boredom away and provided a modicum of physical exercise of which I was glad.

As Nora was the only woman aboard the ship, she thrived on the admiration and kindnesses of the crew. One unfortunate incident occurred some two weeks after our propeller broke. One must take into account that under normal circumstances the crew would have been by now safely home with their relatives and friends if things had gone all right. The air was still bleak and ice cold. The men doing most of the hard work of keeping the ice away were the stokers who were often exposed to the raw weather conditions.

One day our cabin door was suddenly opened and the steward popped his head in and shouted, 'Lock your door!' I locked the door and then went to the window. About seven or eight of the crew were milling round, dancing and shouting on the deck. They were calling in no uncertain language for the Chief Engineer to come out. Apparently they were stone drunk and after somebody's blood. This pandemonium went on for some time, then the hatch at the end of our cabin, which led to the stewards' galley opened and our steward's face appeared. He looked pretty shaken. He told us that some of the stokers had broken into the stores and got at the emergency rum ration. They were completely drunk and anything might happen. All the Officers and the Captain had locked themselves in.

He was pretty scared. We watched through the window again,

and as we looked we saw one big chap walk, or stagger to be correct, straight over the ship's side. He gave a terrific yell as he fell. Instantly, everything was quiet as everyone rushed to the ship's side to peer over – even we rushed out. Normally the ship would have been clear of ice so we expected him to have gone under, the chances of survival in water of such freezing temperature being minimal. To everyone's surprise, he was lying spread-eagled, quite motionless, on a huge ice-floe that had, unnoticed, floated back and now lay against the ship's side. Everyone was sober now and immediate steps were taken to rescue him. They detected faint signs of life when they got him aboard and laid him down in the steward's cabin.

The wireless telegraphist put a call through for medical aid to the Mission Station. I heard afterwards that the Russians had a tremendous row with the Military Mission about the breaking of the radio silence by our telegraphist. Four or five hours later we discerned a black object moving against the whiteness of the distant horizon. It was a reindeer-drawn sleigh. The sleigh came within about a quarter of a mile of the ship and then two bulky figures stepped out, moving from one floe to the other until they came to the clear stretch of water round our ship, from where one of our boats picked them up. When they climbed over the ship's side, I recognised one of them as a Vet Doctor from Archangel.

Her examination of the patient consisted of tapping round his skull with the tips of her fingers. Then taking a pair of scissors from the small cloth bundle she carried, she cut a 'lane' through his hair from forehead to crown, looked at the wound thus bared and gave instructions for the patient to be held firmly and securely while she took out a swab of lint which she soaked with spirit and then swabbed onto the wound. Even though the man remained unconscious with eyes closed, he groaned and struggled, and as he was about sixteen stone they had a job to keep him still. The Doctor then stitched what she could of the gaping wound, and bound his head with lint and bandages that we supplied. Her task finished, she had worked with a kind of set expression all the time, she gave the man two hearty cuffs, one on each side of the face and growled in Russian, 'Phew! To think I have to risk my life for a drunken pig like this!' and then something else which I won't translate.

The Captain and those of the crew around were startled at this behaviour, and I had to diplomatically explain that it was part of the treatment to bring the patient back to consciousness, and that she had said he would soon be all right. Luckily the stoker was up and about the next day as large as life, though a shade more subdued in his manner. Ever since this affair I have had a great deal of admiration and respect for the toughness of the Geordies.

During the weeks that followed, we got confused with days and dates. We seemed to be living in a state of suspended animation with no knowledge of what was going on around us. Eventually our new propeller arrived from England. It had been flown over specially and was delivered to us on about 12 May, 1942. There was, however, still a job to be done before it could be fitted. The remains of the old propeller had to be removed. What had at first been considered a routine task, proved more formidable than our Naval divers had anticipated. I gathered it was so tightly jammed because of the cold that it was impossible to unjam the shaft – apart from the fact that the intense cold of the water only allowed them to submerge for a short time. The Russians, not being at all happy about having a sitting target stuck helpless in the White Sea, offered their assistance, which was accepted.

They sent a couple of their own divers to our ship and after examining the shaft reported that although it might seem impossible, they could do the job by dynamiting the propeller collar off the shaft. It was a technique our chaps were not accustomed to, but the Russians said it would not be the first time they had undertaken this kind of work. The trouble was, we were carrying a load of depth charges and powder for the gun, and as the means of unloading them were not available, they were afraid the explosion might spark them off too. The whole matter was gone into with the Mission and the Russians in Archangel. It became very pressing as the ship was urgently needed. Then it was referred to the Admiralty and Ministry of Transport in London by our Mission for a decision. It took them ten days to decide to let the Russians try it their way. Another homeward bound convoy was already being assembled – the QP 13 and they wanted, if possible, to include us in it.

On about 17 May, 1942, the two Russian divers once more came aboard. There was no doubt, the propeller casing was jammed firmly on the ship's shaft. They worked for about twelve minutes at a time under the water. When they surfaced and came back on the ship, their hands and face looked almost black to me, so deep was the shade of purple. It must have been a cold job. They were, however, fortified by generous tots of British Naval rum that our divers had brought with them. As they smacked their lips it sounded like small arms fire! They were on the job about three hours, including the many necessary breaks. As soon as they were ready to detonate the charge, everybody was ordered to the uttermost tip of the ship's bows, our depth charges having meanwhile been moved from their position at the stern of the ship to a safer place further midships behind the timber stacks.

I think everyone was anticipating a spectacular explosion. But when the charge was detonated all that was heard or felt was a dull thump with the ship swaying ever so slightly. One of the divers descended immediately and soon came up to report that the operation had been successful. Within a few hours, the new propeller had been lowered overboard and fixed into position. After several hours of testing, the Chief Engineer was satisfied enough to report that we could sail again at any time. Everyone felt cheerful at this news, and more so when next morning we awoke to find our ship surrounded by about twenty other ships, with their heliographs signalling away like mad to one another. We knew that once again we would shortly be sailing.

We watched fascinated as the ships slowly took up position. Our own engines began to hum with a steady throb and soon the whole fleet was moving in a northerly direction, our ship sharing the rear end of the formation with three other ships. It was on 21 May, 1942, as our convoy, the homeward bound QP 13, which together with those from Murmansk was to consist of thirty-five ships, began their voyage. We were escorted through the White Sea by two Russian destroyers that moved constantly round our group. By the next day we were out of the White Sea and joined by the other ships from Murmansk with several English destroyers as escorts, and two submarines, one of which was pointed out to me as the *Trident*. The Russian escort then turned back.

The sky was blue, the warm sun shone brightly and the sea was perfectly calm. In a few days we would cross with the Russia-bound PQ 16 which had left Iceland on the same date as ourselves with a similar total of thirty-five ships. They had the protection of several heavy cruisers, a number of destroyers, anti-aircraft ships, armed trawlers, corvettes, and submarines. Soon we would meet them and they would escort us on to Iceland. Meanwhile, as Nora and I leaned over the ship's rail, we could not help feeling proud and reassured at the sight of our own flotilla of ships, albeit they were merchantmen. They stretched far and wide before us and we ploughed on so steadily and in perfect formation that it looked as though nothing could stop us.

One day the ships all around us began exchanging signals rapidly with their heliographs and the word quickly spread that something was amiss. I was called to join the gun crew. We could see a destroyer racing round our convoy darting in and out of the ships: the submarines that had been riding on the surface with us dived. After a few minutes of anxious waiting, a black speck in the sky behind us became visible and revealed itself as a gigantic German Dornier flying boat, with a fantastic wing-span on which could be seen the twelve engines that powered its flight. As we were on the tail-end of the convoy we got a good view of her as she came closer and could even discern figures moving about on her flight deck. The destroyers let fly with their pom-poms, but she kept out of range. We could do nothing with our gun because we couldn't get the elevation. The First Officer instructed me to get Nora to put on her lifebelt as he reckoned the flying boat's job was not to attack us but to signal the submarine pack of our position and we could expect action at any moment. Sure enough, the signals were flashing again and we began to drop our depth charges. One-two-three-four-five and over one would go, a gigantic boiling spout of water would spume into the air behind us and the ship would shake and shudder as though it was falling to pieces.

The sea all around would seem like one vast multi-spouting cauldron as the other ships did the same. We could tell that our course was being changed by the white trail of foam from the para-vanes which revolved on leads from the stern of each ship. These paravanes were quite important because they acted as guides, starting from the leading ship to those following on behind in the line;

their effectiveness was especially important at night when the churning foam took on an almost phosphorescent glow which could be easily discerned in the darkness.

To the officers, 'Wait for it, the fireworks can start any time now!' we sailed on, the Dornier having been left behind. It was now dusk. I looked at Nora strolling round the deck near by, quite calm, cool, and totally unconcerned with all the bustle around her. She was wearing the life jacket, which she had only put on after strong insistence from me. It made her look too fat she said. I muttered a silent prayer to myself. We slept in our clothes that night and every night afterwards, dozing fitfully whenever we could. One night we became aware that the steady throbbing of the ship's engines had stopped. We got up and went on deck. We could not see a thing. Even the deck rail was undiscernible. We were shrouded in a thick blanket of fog. It was quite eerie. We made our way to the officers' mess room which was deserted, and waited a while. The steward was the first to appear with mugs of hot coffee. We refused the offer of food. Later one of the officers joined us and from him I gathered what had happened.

It appeared that the fog came so suddenly and thickly it had been impossible to make out any signals from the other ships. We had also lost sight of the paravane trail. To make matters worse, the Captain had fallen ill and was unconscious in his cabin. Only the steward, the First Officer and the Chief Engineer were allowed to see him. They had decided to stop the ship's engines for fear of being detected by lurking submarines. It was not known how long the fog bank would last, so we were drifting along helplessly, hoping for the best. Such was our plight and it continued for several days. When the fog did eventually lift, we emerged once again into bright sunlight, to find ourselves quite alone with not another ship in sight. I recalled the words of *The Ancient Mariner*, 'Like a painted ship, upon a painted ocean'. It felt just like that! The engines were started up again and we began to move. I went along to the navigation room. Our officers were busily engaged plotting out our position and movement from the charts on the table. They looked very serious and puzzled. Another anxious day and night went by as we forged steadily onwards. Once we were called to action stations as the look-out picked up a black speck in the sky which turned out to be the Dornier again. It circled round at a respectable distance and after some time flew off. Again we waited, keeping a close watch for the expected submarine attack and tell-tale tracks of torpedoes. We zig-zagged on for several hours, the tension mounting with each passing hour. We ran into a fine mist which suddenly turned into thick impenetrable fog and again our engines were stopped. Once more the fog suddenly lifted to reveal we were alone with not a ship in sight. Again we set off on a course that even our officers were not sure about.

After a couple of days we were again picked up by the damned Dornier which fluttered round us like a huge black bird of ill-omen. Once again came the call 'to action stations' and there were many hurried consultations in the chart room, the Captain still being very ill. How I silently prayed! Nora, meanwhile, seemingly unperturbed, was busy with furrowed brows studying English to which she devoted much of her time with patience and diligence. Yet again, as though in answer to my prayers, we were suddenly enshrouded in a thick blanket of silencing fog. The engines stopped once more and again we drifted helplessly. The days since we had left Archangel had now turned into weeks; we had lost all track of time. It was terrifying trying to peer through the fog, yet we dare not relax our vigilance. How long we remained sightless in this bank of fog I do not remember. The awful memory of its lifting was to haunt me throughout my life in recurrent nightmares whenever I came under stress.

While standing at the ship's rail leaning over, trying to penetrate the fog that surrounded us, I became aware of several figures on either side of me, quite still and silent, elbows apart, resting on the rails, occasionally they would spit reflectively into the waters below. They were some of the stokers who had come up for a breather. They too stared into the thick mist. There were two on either side of me with sweat rags bound round their foreheads which gave them a most peculiar appearance. By now the fog was getting lighter and it would swirl in patches round these silent staring figures beside me. Their features would seem to recede and then come forward at me as though they were ghosts constantly disappearing and then re-appearing. I felt a sudden feeling of disembodiment, as though it was not me but someone else, looking down upon the strange mist-filled scene. It was then that looking over the side I became aware we were cutting into a floating island of dead fish of all shapes and sizes, floating motionless, white bellies upwards – to my horror I could discern here and there among them, the half submerged floating corpses of men – the waves washing over their white faces, jaws agape; their hair awash around their heads as they bobbed up and down. I motioned my companions and pointed out to them the horrible sight below us. They said nothing – just nodded their heads and turned away to re-commence their duties. It all happened so quickly, we were once again in the bright sunlight surging forward with ever-increasing power over a sea that was calm, deep green and beautiful.

Still feeling dazed and somewhat detached I returned to our cabin. As the long watchful day ended and whilst Nora lay fast asleep in the stillness of the night, I looked down upon her calm untroubled face and scribbled the following lines upon a scrap of paper:

> I am alone, quite alone,
> And all things touch me not,
> For I am as nothing,
> In utter nothingness,
> Where time, endless, boundless time,
> That has no beginning or end,
> Fetters my restless soul
> To the void of spaceless destiny.
>
> 4th July, 1942, somewhere in the Arctic Sea

It just about described my feelings at the time, for it seemed my life was set upon a course already charted by fate and the extraordinary events that had taken place and those to come were a prescribed destiny.

During this period we had been very short of food, having been unable to re-provision before joining the second convoy. We had bread, tea, tinned milk, sugar, coffee and cocoa. The rest of the meals were made up of a concoction of various ingredients including oatmeal. We had no meats or vegetables, but the worst shortage was lack of tobacco and cigarettes. This was something the men felt very keenly about as their nerves were on edge. When the steward came to me and asked if I happened to have any more of my own left, which I had not, he explained his dilemma. I asked him if by any chance he happened to have such a thing as snuff in his stores. To my surprise he said he had about sixteen pounds of it. I told him that as good snuff is composed of over seventy per cent tobacco dust, he could use it with the used tea leaves, which after being dried could be mixed with the snuff and used as tobacco for rolling cigarettes. As there were plenty of cigarette papers in store it proved quite successful in bringing some relief to the situation and was better than nothing.

We sailed on for another couple of days without anything more untoward happening. The ship's officers were anxiously poring over their charts, convinced we were somewhere near Iceland by this time, when the shout came, 'Land, Ahoy!' I could not see any land, but they could. A corvette also speedily came into view and after a lot of signalling, we followed the corvette which led us along a high rocky coastline into an inlet. This was Seydisfjord on the east coast of Iceland, some five hundred miles from Reykjavik on the west coast of Iceland, which should have been our desti-nation. A boom across the mouth was lifted and we sailed into the fjord, where three destroyers were lined up, their funnels smoking, showing that they were at action stations. As we steamed in be-tween the steep sides of the fjord I noticed a small town, or I should say, village, at the end of it running down to the jetty at which we would land.

As we got nearer, I discerned a little picturesque church, painted white, with a bright red roof and green spire standing at the end of the village high on the rocky slope. I vowed to myself that as soon as I got ashore the first thing I would do would be to get to that church and offer a silent prayer to God for bringing us safely through. We docked, and leaving the ship's officers to do their job, asked the Naval Embarkation Officer for permission to go ashore with Nora. This was granted. Waiting on the quay was a YMCA representative by the name of Ernie Corkhill who ran the Forces' canteen there. He made us extremely welcome and looked after Nora while I made my way to the church. It was an uphill climb. The doors of this little chapel were open and I heard the strains of an organ playing as I entered. What the organist was playing I do not know, but it was the sweetest sound in the world. Silently I entered and went down on my knees, covering my face with my hands in deep meditative thanks to God for the mercy He had shown. I stayed a few minutes and then made my way down to the YMCA canteen. Nora had already eaten.

Ernie cooked me a couple of eggs and several rashers of bacon, which I washed down with a big mug of tea. The meal tasted great. Nora badly needed some clothes by now, she had been wearing mine since we left Archangel. I had no money, only a cheque book. Ernie insisted that I was not to bother – he would see me and settle up in England if I would let him know my address. He took Nora to a ladies outfitters where she got a dress and other things and we returned to the ship, which was to leave for Reykjavik the next morning, 9 July 1942, in the company of an armed trawler for part of the way.

The journey to Reykjavik was uneventful. We had a clear, smooth passage, hugging the rocky coastline all the way. On the night of 11 July, 1942, we docked alongside some badly battered ships in the harbour. Nora and I were greeted very warmly by Wing-Commander Leeroy Brown, a veteran Canadian Pilot from the First World War. He was the RAF embarkation officer and did everything possible to make us feel at home. He became one of my greatest friends. We were provided with a room in a neat, clean little hotel and had meals in the RAF Officers' mess. To all we were a source of wonder as the news of the *Empire Stevenson*'s adventurous journey became known. I cannot remember much of Iceland and would dearly like to see it properly sometime. The thing that really caught Nora's interest was the quaint old-fashioned attire of the Icelandic women in their national costume which had been very evident in Seydisfjord.

On 12 July 1942, Wing-Commander Leeroy Brown informed me that he had arranged a transfer for Nora and myself to an American troopship, the USS *Siboney* which he reckoned would get us home quicker, as the *Empire Stevenson* had to be delayed for overhaul and re-fuelling. It was then that I heard from him of the terrible and tragic sequence of events that had been taking place whilst our own ship had been blindly zig-zagging its course alone across the Arctic Ocean. Cut off as we were from any means of communication, owing to the strict necessity for radio silence, we had no means of knowing what carnage and destruction was taking place around us.

It transpired that our convoy, the homeward bound QP 13, sailing on without us had crossed with the Russia-bound convoy PQ 16 off Bear Island and although dogged by enemy aircraft had managed to reach the comparative safety of the waters to the north of Iceland without mishap. However, it was there that tragedy overtook them. The weather suddenly deteriorated. A wicked north-easterly gale sprang up. The blinding rain that followed reduced visibility to a few hundred yards. The commanding officer of the minesweeper, *Niger*, sighting an iceberg in the distance, apparently mistook it for the North Cape of Iceland and altering the course of his section of the convoy led it straight into a British minefield. The *Niger* itself was the first to hit a mine and quickly sank with heavy loss of life, including that of the commander. Within a brief space of time a further four ships struck mines and sank with two more ships sustaining serious damage. One of those lost was the Russian ship *Rodina* carrying the wives and families of Soviet diplomats, who were sailing to join their husbands stationed in London.

Whilst all this was going on, the PQ 16, on having crossed with our convoy safely, and continuing on its final leg to Russia, also met with disaster. They were picked up by enemy aircraft and submarines and seven of its ships were sent to the bottom. The losses here might have been greater still but for two important factors. First, the onset of appalling weather which included dense fog and secondly, the withdrawal of the enemy attacking forces to prepare for an all-out attack on a second outward bound convoy which was on its way from Iceland to Russia and about which the German Intelligence service agency had obtained information.

This was the PQ 17, consisting of thirty-four heavily laden ships that had already left Iceland on 27 June, 1942. The outcome of the attack on this convoy was a massacre. Twenty-three of its ships were sent to the bottom. Scattered and helpless in those icy seas, they had become sitting targets for a merciless enemy.

It was much later when we were back in England that I was to learn the ultimate fate that befell our own ship, a ship that was barely one year old.

Arriving home on 28 July, 1942, she was refitted, loaded and sent off from Hull to join another Russia-bound convoy. This was to be her last voyage – the official communique about her read:

> The steamship *Empire Stevenson* on a voyage from Hull to north Russia was torpedoed by a German aircraft, blew up and sank on September 13th, 1942, off the North Cape. All on board were lost, 41 crew and 19 gunners. . . .

On 13 July, 1942, Nora and I boarded the American SS *Siboney* from Reykjavik. She was a very fast converted lake boat of about 10,000 tons carrying supplies to Britain. We were accompanied by a corvette for the first part of the journey which then turned back. The most astonishing thing was the food we had aboard. Every kind of meat and poultry was served, even roast turkey and cranberry sauce. Fresh fruit including melon, and the most super ice-cream. I had not seen such food for ages, and I was not to see the like of it either for more years than I care to remember. Being a good sailor I was able to enjoy my meals to the full, but Nora, together with many of the crew, was affected by the stormy weather, and hardly ate anything. The ship rolled immensely, and being a converted lake boat with very little draught, the mountainous Icelandic seas made her behave in the most fantastic fashion.

We had only one submarine alarm and everyone was ordered on deck. Nora was so ill at the time that she could not get up, so I stayed below with her in the cabin and we held hands. Luckily nothing happened.

It was on the night of 16 July, 1942, that we slowly steamed into Gourock. We had spent nearly eighty days on those Arctic Seas and now our journey was ended. The dimmed lights on the quayside were a grim reminder that the war was not yet over, yet it mattered not, we were safely home at last. Whether we landed in England, Ireland, Wales or Scotland made little difference, it was still home.

Seventeen eventful years had elapsed since I had sailed from

London to seek my fortune, now I was home again, no fortune, but with a bride who had faced a thousand perils for the sake of the love she bore me, and as we stepped ashore we stopped and embraced one another for a few fleeting moments, full of the pent-up emotions that overwhelmed us. The whole world seemed to stand still and as our lips met in one lingering kiss, the muffled blast of a distant ship's siren seemed to echo our unspoken thoughts. We were indeed home at last.

> Breathes there the man, with soul so dead,
> Who never to himself hath said,
> This is my own, my native land!

Lay of the Last Minstrel
Sir Walter Scott

EPILOGUE

Gourock, on the south bank of the Firth of Clyde, was to be the first British land on which John and Nora alighted after three months at sea in July 1942. From then onwards their lives faced different and in some ways more complicated challenges.

Upon moving to London, they found accommodation at 52 Parliament Hill Mansions, NW5. John was allowed to postpone his National Service duties until after the birth of their first son John junior (January 18th, 1943).

On May 1943, John received his certificate of Conduct and Ability for Civilians, which covered his employment for the Air Attaché in Moscow, and later when allocated to No 30 Military Mission to the USSR in Kuibyshev and Archangel (August 1940-March 1942). The Air Ministry described his conduct as 'good' and his work 'completely satisfactory.' With such credentials, John immediately enlisted in the Royal Air Force Civilian Technical Corps, joining the Army's Intelligence Corps in May, 1943.

Already pregnant with their second child, Nora, and their new-born son John junior, moved to 7 Harrington Square, Mornington Crescent, London, renting a small two-room flat on the second floor. Soon after, Nora began to tire of the rigours of war time London, and chose to join John at his encampment in Derby. Nearby Willersley Castle, in Matlock, was used as a maternity hospital during WWII. 4,000 well-blessed babies were born into such regal surroundings – their second son, Peter was one of them.

John was away much of the time and, like many couples during the war, they snatched moments of intimacy whenever they could. Despite such limitations, Nora soon fell pregnant with their third child. She had given up going to the bomb shelter in Harrington Square Gardens opposite her flat. There they stayed, in what Nora described as a slum, throughout the war, enduring the bombings. In June 1945, their third son Leeroy was born in Islington Hospital, London.

On August 26 1946, John received his Release Leave Certificate from the Intelligence Corps Military Dispersal Unit. It states: *'He has proved a hard-working, conscientious and loyal member of the staff, and has always been very cheerful and willing. He is very intelligent and capable, works well without supervision. An industrious honest and sober man, confident and reliable.'* Military conduct: *'EXEMPLARY.'*

Luckily for John and Nora, they were allocated one of the newly erected Council prefabs on the edge of Hampstead Heath, London. In September 1946, the Murray family moved to their 'people's palace' at 120a Savernake Road, NW3, to start their new life. This was all the more auspicious for it would allow John to house his newly-arrived parents in their old Harrington Square flat. They had been interned on the island of Kythnos for the duration of the war, enduring years of starvation under the Germans and Italians. Only through the efforts of the Red Cross had it been possible to locate them and arrange their safe passage back to Britain. When John met them off the boat he was appalled and upset by their withered physical appearance.

After the war John reunited with his two brothers and set up a printing enterprise, having obtained a licence to use the new offset litho printing technology. Sadly they were forbidden from importing the machines due to severe currency restrictions. The Attlee Government prioritised essential imports that used sterling.

Despite investing large sums of money into the business, John could not find anyone in England to manufacture the American offset printer for which he had the sole licence. As the business began to fail, his brother Nicholas went his own way, leaving John and his youngest brother Dimitri to pick up the pieces of their faltering enterprise.

Meanwhile, Nora had written her memoirs. These were soon picked up by the literary agency Curtis Brown and turned into her successful book - *I Spied for Stalin*. Upon its release, and subsequent translation into seven languages, Nora became an instant celebrity.

By 1951, John's printing business had failed, leaving him unemployed for the next 18 months. During this time, the family

177

lived off the earnings from Nora's book. She revelled in her new found celebrity status, meeting film stars and other notables. While travelling abroad, a Hungarian nanny was employed to look after the three boys.

Around 1953, John eventually found a job as a general hand, working the nightshift in Wall's food factory in Acton, London. Things became more difficult for him during these years due to the additional need to care for his sick parents. John's mother died in August 1952; his father died a year later, causing their son great distress.

For John's family, the highlight of his work (besides a regular wage), was the ice-cream and sausages he brought home to supplement their meagre pantry. John found the nature of his work arduous. By 1955 it had taken its toll on his health, forcing him to give up his factory job, even though he had been promoted to manager.

At this time, all was not well on the home front. With little money coming in, a somewhat jaundiced John indignantly found himself queuing both to find work and to receive social security handouts. The hardships conspired to make life intolerable, especially for Nora. She resented her domestic existence in the prefab and their children became tragically neglected. With Nora often out, John found coping increasingly difficult. In the summer of 1956, he and Nora separated in a brutally swift manner. John and the boys returned home from a two-week camping holiday in Folkestone to find it deserted. Everything was as they left it, with rotting food on the table and unwashed dishes. John was distraught and angry. Without her he was lost, gripped by a fear almost to the point of wanting to end his life. A doctor friend talked him round, prescribing anti-depressants which he took for a short time.

While barely coping with three boys, John managed to work as a clerical officer in Holloway Prison. Although the pay as a low grade civil servant was meagre, it would be enough to keep the family afloat. With persistence and courage, John lasted a year but unfortunately suffered a slipped disc that left him unable to move. He was taken to the Royal Northern hospital, London, where he remained for one month. The boys were left to fend for themselves.

178

By then, John junior had won a scholarship to the City of London School. Peter and Leeroy simply stayed in the prefab for several months until they were picked up by the school authorities. This intervention resulted in their attendance at Haverstock Hill School in Chalk Farm from February 1957.

John and the three boys moved into Welford Court in August 1959. By this time Nora and her new partner Ismail Petrushevski had moved into their own flat in Harrington Square.

John's back continued to give him problems, leaving him hospitalised for a further three months. The boys, now aged 14, 15, and 16 evolved a plan to fend for themselves, sharing the household chores such as cooking and cleaning. During this time, the flat became a magnet for their school friends, especially those suffering from family problems or issues of their own. On his return from hospital John never objected to the many and varied characters using Welford Court as a refuge, including drug addicts, abused kids and those with mental health problems. John explained to his children that given the horrors he had experienced during the war, any problems encountered at their home could never compare.

John later wrote: 'I used to keep an open house for their student friends, regardless of sex, creed, religion or whether they sat on their heads and blew fire. The time was the sixties and all I can say is that these students kept me young and I suppose in a way encouraged the idea which eventually changed my life.'

In 1961, one of the guests staying at the flat showed John a job advertisement for a position at London Zoo. His application was successful, and he was taken on as a clerk. This success helped to restore his dignity, drive and determination. He loved his life there and would speak with such pride about helping to maintain the world's most famous Victorian zoo. He spent many happy years there until he retired in 1973, at the age of 65.

With his three sons now fully-grown, and all benefitting from a university education, John felt ready to start life again. And what better way to reinvent himself, than entering academia too? Accepted at Nottingham University to study history, he was placed in Cripps Hall of residence with students of his own sons' ages. His

179

instant popularity was attested by the fact that his fellow students clubbed together to help pay his fees so that he could continue into the second year. For his third year, he was recommended by the University to manage a student hostel in London during the summer. With such support, he completed three years at university, culminating in him writing his autobiographical book *A Spy Called Swallow*, published in 1978.

In the summer of 1980, John's sons treated him to a trip on the QE2 to visit Leeroy, who had by then emigrated to Canada. During the five-day voyage, John became something of a celebrity, giving talks on his experiences during the war and signing copies of his book. An American lady, from Buffalo New York, was so taken by the 72-year-old man that she persuaded him to tour the United States with her. They spent three months travelling around the USA together, and on his return to England, she followed.

After several months in the UK, John and his new partner, aged 55, returned to Buffalo. John stayed for two years, living the American life while trying to win over her petulant 15-year-old son. His winning tickets to see the Rolling Stones in Toronto was the one thing that finally bridged the sizable generation gap.

By 1986, John realised that his partner was not only struggling with alcoholism but mental health problems too. Here was someone he could not help, despite his best attempts to do so. He returned to England, and to his flat in Camden.

With John's return, Welford Court once again ran an open-house policy with family friends, and friends of friends coming from all over the world. People from America, Chile, Brazil, China and Europe would stay for a few days, sharing their customs and cuisine with John, now widely known as 'Pops.' In return he would hold court with his colourful war-time adventures, stories about his life in the Balkans and Guy the gorilla at London Zoo.

For John's sons, he remained their lynchpin in London, and somewhere they could stay when visiting town on business, holidays with their children or just to hang out seeing friends. John was an integral part of their family friend network.

Many of the boys' friends also knew Nora too and visited her when invited. Throughout this period she was curious about her ex-husband's life. Indeed, from the time John went to university, she had taken a surreptitious interest in his life, initially from curiosity and then as an onlooker. She had been given a copy of his book in 1979 (which she secretly treasured).

Likewise, John kept an eye on Nora from a distance. Hearing of her hysterectomy in 1988, he sent her a large bunch of red roses anonymously. He learnt from the boys about how she was coping, often enquiring if she needed anything. On learning that Nora was admitted to hospital in May 1989, John became more concerned. In early June he went with Peter to the hospital, but did not enter the ward. Unknown to the family at that time, Nora had been diagnosed with terminal cancer.

When Peter returned, devastated by the site of his frail mother, John asked if he should go in to see her too. Peter Just shook his head. Sensing the severity of the situation, John went in regardless. He wrote: 'I felt a terrible sinking feeling in the pit of my stomach, as I knew there must be something terribly wrong with Nora. The ward seemed very quiet and empty as I entered; there were no visitors at that hour and the nurses were heavily occupied in various corners of the room. I walked down the centre of the ward looking left and right at the beds. The patients seemed old and tired and I wondered if I would recognise Nora. I hadn't seen her in 30 years and it was possible she'd changed a good deal in that time. Seeing one bed with someone lying on their side, their back towards me, I tentatively approached whispering 'Nora' to which she replied, 'Johniks …is that you Johnichka.' As she struggled to get up to face me, I was appalled by her appearance, she looked so ill, all the life seemed to have drained from her. I gently kissed her lips, they were so dry and parched. Hugging her close I buried my face into her outstretched arms. We held each other tightly but gently.'

Crying, Nora asked for forgiveness.

'Ah, Noryshka, there's nothing to forgive,' John replied gently stroking her hand. 'It's you who should forgive me for leaving you alone for so long.

'The tears rolled down our cheeks, 'I love you, I love you! I've always loved you!' was all we could keep saying to one another.'

181

John would be reunited with Nora from then onwards and understood only too well when she wanted to go home.

Over the next few weeks the family was reunited, including Jan, Nora's partner at the time. John and Jan took it in turns to nurse and comfort Nora. John junior had taken six months leave from his Professorship at Toulouse University, France and along with Peter provided much needed support.

In his grief following Nora's death, John wrote the following, bringing closure to one of the century's most remarkable love stories, entitled: *Reconciliation and the Last Flight of the Swallow*.

'As I sat at her bedside she suddenly became agitated and tried to speak, she waved her arms pointing to the other side of the bed where a small table stood laden with what I thought were very large books. I nodded my head in the direction she pointed and asked if it was one of the books she wanted. 'Da, Da-a,' she whispered.

'I walked round to the other side of the bed and lifted up the top book, it was heavy, it was not a book at all, but a large leather-bound photo album. Returning to my seat with the album she stretched out her hand to open it for me, but she was so weak the effort was too much. Leaning over the bed I opened it. Turning the pages, I saw that each leaf contained an enlarged print of photos taken of ourselves and the children during the early happy years of our marriage.

'I gazed at them with awe and astonishment. I had long since forgotten about them, I did not know even that she had kept them.

'As we silently turned page after page, the tears welled up in my eyes.

'Ah, Norushka!' I said. 'So you did remember after all.' She nodded her head at my remark.

'Then she did something that bought back vividly the old happier days.

'As I leaned over to kiss her, she slowly stroked the side of my face, just like in the old times when I was tired and worried. She never spoke, she always just stroked my cheek gently and slowly.

'This time her grey-green eyes looked steadily at me, they sparkled with a strange light.'

'It was then I understood; this was the moment she had been waiting for throughout all the long years of our separation. She began to say something in Russian, but her voice, so low and feeble was beyond my comprehension, the accompanying wan smile she gave me was, however, one of quiet triumph.

'Slowly I stood up, closing the album. I walked round the bed to replace it on the table. As I did so, I saw she had folded her hands across her breast, I heard a soft drawn-out sigh and as I looked, her eyes momentarily fluttered and then closed - never to open again.

'It was The Swallow's last flight – but she left behind a broken heart.'

www.gbpublishing.co.uk

I Spied For Stalin: Freedom's Sacrifice by **Nora Murray**

(Companion Title to *A Spy Called Swallow: An Enduring Love Story)*

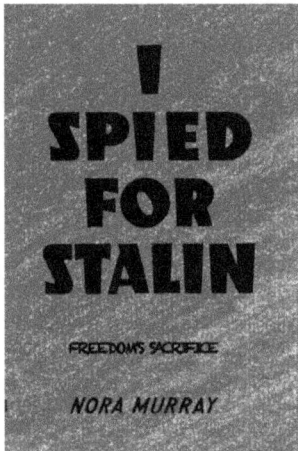

This is Nora's story leading up to and following on from her encounter with John Murray. Republished by GB Publishing.org, in similar fashion to *A Spy Called Swallow: An Enduring Love Story,* a prologue and epilogue is added by her sons Leeroy and Peter Murray.